Bicentennial History

of

Union Presbyterian Church

Bicentennial Book Committee

LEONA SCOTT	JAMES STRUNK
OTTO PERSON	RON PARRISH
WILLIAM TIDBALL	CHUCK PUHLMAN
R. DONALD SCOTT	BERTHA PERSON

Photograph Chairman
RON PARRISH

Bicentennial History
of
UNION PRESBYTERIAN CHURCH

Robinson Township, Pennsylvania
Pittsburgh Presbytery

1794 - 1994

Compiled and written by the
Bicentennial Book Committee

PROVIDENCE HOUSE PUBLISHERS
FRANKLIN, TENNESSEE

Copyright 1993
Union Presbyterian Church
Robinson Township, Pennsylvania

All rights reserved. Written permission must be secured from the publisher to use or reproduce any part of this book, except for brief quotations in critical reviews and articles.

Printed in the United States of America.

ISBN 0-881576-15-9

Published by
PROVIDENCE HOUSE PUBLISHERS
Presbyterian Custom Publishing
P.O. Box 158, Franklin, Tennessee 37065

Contents

Foreword and Acknowledgments	Bicentennial Book Committee	7
1. Early Families and Heritage	Leona C. Scott	9
2. Land and Buildings	Leona C. Scott	26
3. Church Officers	Leona C. Scott	32
4. Activities and Organizations	James Strunk	39
5. Music Program	Leona C. Scott	56
6. Schism	Otto Person	59
7. Denominational Mergers	Leona C. Scott	67
8. Pastors	William Tidball Leona C. Scott	71
Afterword; Through the Years	Leona C. Scott	81
Appendices		
A. Ministers from Union Church	Charles Puhlman	89
B. Daughter Congregations	Charles Puhlman	91
C. Missionaries from Union Church	Charles Puhlman	93
D. Union National Shrine	R. Donald Scott	95
E. Church Officers (1794–1993)	James Strunk Bertha Person	125

Third church building, used from 1856 to 1899.

Present church structure as dedicated June 9, 1901.

Foreword and Acknowledgments

Union Presbyterian Church of Robinson Township was established in 1794. The first history was written by Samuel S. Glass in 1894 and revised in 1944. A short "Retrospective" was published in 1929. The purpose of this history is to enrich the previous history by offering some new material based on court records, Associate Reformed Presbyterian minutes and publications, other church records and Union Church family histories. Events taking place after the 1944 edition will be added.

Documentation of the organizing events at Union is difficult. Few of the oldest churches can give the date or circumstances of their organization or produce session records. Union's oligraphic records begin with Session minutes dated February 20, 1835. Men were too busy to write. They were making history carving homes for themselves and their large families in a hostile wilderness.

The contribution of Union Church's Scotch-Irish founders and the impact of their culture and beliefs in shaping the growth of Robinson Township is incalculable. They furnished leaders in civil affairs; they were found on school boards and in teaching positions; they were justices of the peace. They were patriotic as measured by the number of Revolutionary War veterans buried in Union Cemetery. Their children were nourished on religion and in education, for it was important for a good Presbyterian to be able to read the Bible and the Psalter. The Scotch-Irish were industrious as measured by the size of the farms, or "plantations", as they were called at that time.

Acknowledgments in documenting and researching this history must be given to early writers of Union's history and to Rev. J. W. English, author of the first history of Robinson Run U.P. Church. Dr. Reid Stewart, present pastor of the Dormont Presbyterian Church, has researched and written scholarly articles about the Reformed Churches in Western Pennsylvania. He was generous with his time, his expertise and his library. The Bicentennial Book Committee is indebted to Joan Ecoff for placing the manuscript into the computer and for her time and patience when corrections and additions were made.

Church interior, 1894 Centennial.

1894 Centennial celebration.

1
Early Families and Heritage

Founders of the Associate Reformed Church later to be named "Union," had a distinctive character which was molded in their Scotch/Irish heritage. They were Scottish and English people who had gone to Ireland to take up the confiscated estates of Irish rebels. The Scottish king encouraged his Presbyterian subjects to do this. The migration began in the early part of the 17th century and was extensive. These Presbyterians settled in Northern Ireland and became known as *Ulstermen* or *Scotch/Irish* in America. It has been written that they were thrifty and intelligent. After successfully establishing homes for themselves in Ireland, religious persecution began at the hands of a new king of England. The native Irish also succeeded in killing a few thousand of the Scotch/Irish.

The promise of security, opportunity and prosperity stimulated many of them to emigrate to America. Migration began about 1700 and continued for 40 to 60 years. They came into the port of Philadelphia or to New Castle, Delaware. A large number of these emigrants settled in Eastern Pennsylvania, in Lancaster, York and Cumberland Counties. Perhaps they were attracted to Pennsylvania by the fame of the colony for religious liberty and for its fertile soil. About the same time, German immigrants were also arriving to take up farming in those areas. Early records indicate that the two groups were not entirely compatible. Just before the Revolutionary War, the Scotch-Irish began a migration to the Western frontier. Land had been purchased by the government from the Indians enabling pioneers to obtain large tracts at thrifty prices.

Land was cheap, but it was heavily timbered, damp and cold. Game was abundant. Herds of buffalo and elk wandered through the woods. Indians were still lurking about. The innate qualities of self-reliance, ingenuity and improvisation of these hardy pioneers were invaluable in carving out homes in the wilderness and in facing Indian attacks.

For the brief period they farmed in Eastern Pennsylvania, some of the future members of Union shared the same Reformed Presbyterian minister, Rev. John Cuthbertson. He kept an extensive diary of his activities and some names of Union's early members can be found in that diary. He mentions Spiers, McCormick, McFadden, Scotts and Walker. It is certain that some of the founders of Union knew each other before arriving here. On journeys back East to pick-up supplies, they spread the good news about opportunities on the frontier, so their friends gradually joined them. Their powerful cultural bonds were again reinforced.

Former neighbors in the East and companions on the journey westward met at Church. They welcomed the Sabbath for the opportunity to worship and to chat. The Church played a big part in meeting social needs and matchmaking. Genealogies of Union Church members prove that point.

We can begin to trace the religious lives and homes of some of Union's original families because they are mentioned in Rev. John Cuthbertson's diary as part of his scattered congregations in Lancaster County. He writes of visiting Isaac and Gabriel Walker and their families; he marries and baptizes the family of Benjamin McCormick as well as that of Samuel Scott. Gradually these families crossed the mountains and settled in Allegheny County (then part of Washington County) and purchased land. More Presbyterian families joined them

In 1789, the McMichael brothers, the Walker brothers and Samuel Phillips signed the call for the first minister to Montours Church. All later became very early members of Union Church. In fact, Isaac Walker petitioned Monongahela Presbytery for a "supply of preaching" on February 6, 1794, in behalf of this (later Union) congregation.

Land records, early tax records, Revolutionary War records and Union Cemetery graves prove the existence of a number of Union's early families in the area by 1774-90. In addition to the Walkers and the McMichaels, there were William Marks, John Hall, John Nichols, William McCoy, Thomas Thornberry, Hugh McCurdy, John McFadden, Hugh McCormick, William Hall, James Spier, John Lorain, Benjamin McCormick, John, Samuel and Jonathan Phillips. All of these households were large for there were many children. Children were an important requisite on the frontier. They assisted on the farm and provided assurance that family names and traditions would continue.

Union's first history, written in 1894 by Samuel Glass offers brief sketches of some families. We believe our new book should reprint those vignettes.

GABRIEL & ISAAC WALKER

The Walker brothers came from Lancaster County where they were members of Rev. John Cuthbertson's Congregation. Gabriel Walker married Rev. Cuthbertson's "bound girl", Margaret Bell. Three Walker brothers came to Western Pennsylvania in 1772, and purchased about two thousand acres of land, formerly Tomahawk Claims, on Robinson Run. They located near the present site of Walker's Mills. Isaac Walker was a member of Session from the organization of the congregation until his death in 1812. He is buried in Union Cemetery. Both Isaac and Gabriel Walker were arrested by Washington's Army in the fall of 1794 for their participation in the Whiskey Rebellion. They were marched to Philadelphia and held for trial. On May 12, 1795, they were released. It was very common for frontiersmen to have stills on their "plantations", for this was a lucrative business in Western Pennsylvania.

WILLIAM MARKS, SR.

He was one of the first Ruling Elders in Union. He served until his death and is buried in Union Cemetery.

SAMUEL & JONATHAN PHILLIPS

These brothers, originally from Ireland, came to this area before the Revolutionary War, for both are veterans of that War. They purchased vast lands in Robinson Township. Jonathan Phillips was one of the first Ruling Elders and served until his death. Later, Jonathan's and Samuel's sons served as elders.

SAMUEL STEWART

The Stewart family came from Carlisle, Cumberland County, to Findlay Township in Allegheny County. Mr. Stewart was one of the second set of elders to serve.

JAMES McMICHAEL FAMILY

James and his wife, Priscilla, brought their family to this area perhaps as early as 1779. His sons, Isaac and John, were active members of the Church. Both were elders. Isaac is mentioned in Monongahela Presbytery minutes as attending meetings in 1794, 1808 and 1812. John attended as a Ruling Elder in 1812. John was also a Justice of the Peace in the area. In a deposition before Allegheny County Court, June 9, 1834, he claimed the "Union Congregation employed me to purchase of John Wolf five acres of land for the purpose of erecting a house for public worship", between the years 1790 and 1796. Three daughters of James and Priscilla married Church members, John Young, Sr., William Marks and John McFadden. John, Isaac and their father, James were Revolutionary War Veterans.

ISAAC GLASS

This family came to Western Pennsylvania in the 1790's. Descendants of Isaac, Samuel and William were prominent and faithful elders. The Glass family intermarried with the Samuel Scotts, the McCormicks, the Walkers, the Stewarts, the Speers and the Phillips.

WILLIAM AND JOHN HALL

The Halls owned a large farm in Robinson Township. William, Sr. and his son, John served in The Revolutionary War. The warrant for their farm of 300 acres was adjacent to Union Church. They named their acreage "Pine Knot".

JAMES SPIER

The Spier (Spear - Speer) family accompanied by sons, Andrew and James, came from Maryland in 1765 and purchased 322 acres, calling it "New Design" in what is now Kennedy Township. Many members of this family have been active in Union's Congregation. Alexander and later, Clayton, were lifelong elders.

MCCOY FAMILY

There were at least four land warrants granted to the McCoy family in Robinson Township. William, Jr. was an elder in this Congregation.

William, Sr. and his brother, John, served in the Revolutionary War.

SAMUEL SCOTT

Samuel and his wife, Elizabeth Wilson, moved to Robinson Township from Washington County. They were devout members of John Cuthbertson's Congregation and their children were baptized by him at the "Forks of Yough" settlement in 1779. In September 1794, Samuel Scott signed the Amnesty pledging that he would abide by the Excise Tax placed on spirituous liquors by the U.S. Government. Our early history tells us that his son, Samuel Scott was an elder, and very punctual and faithful in the performance of every duty. His pew in the church was seldom empty. He was a man of kindly disposition, though of a somewhat retiring nature. He was ordained March 4, 1869 and served until his death seventeen years later.

BENJAMIN MCCORMICK

The McCormick family were also members of Rev. Cuthbertson's congregation in Lancaster County. He came to Moon Township in 1774 and settled on a farm of 600 acres. This family has also served prominent roles in the history of the Church.

There were other families, too, which made up Union's early Congregation; the above-mentioned appear to form a nucleus. They were intensely religious. Their Bibles and Psalters, along with sturdy rifles were carried across the mountain trails into the unknown wilderness. Ulstermen in Western Pennsylvania capitalized upon self-reliance required for survival. They were bold, sturdy and industrious men, sharp at religious controversy and not strongly attached to any government - royal or proprietary. Any religious divisions occurring in the East were carried across the mountains into Western Pennsylvania. These settlers held tenaciously to the faith of their Scottish heritage and refused to form connections with other churches.

A good example of Presbyterian rivalry can be cited since Montours Presbyterian Church is 1-1/2 miles from Union and was organized in 1788. There were no signs of open hostility, but there was competition for members. Families intermarried and then chose one Church or the other. There are instances of members leaving one Church and affiliating with the other.

It is certain that the founders of Union Church shared similar religious background and worshiped in prayer groups or met for informal Bible study sometime before 1793. Formal organization was not essential in those days. They no doubt gathered in someone's log house or in a grove of trees. Their spiritual needs were met through knowledge of the Bible and wise words or counsel of an earnest layman. Some pioneers could read the Bible and were able to write. They became the leaders and teachers until the Associate Reformed Church sent them ministers from Scotland.

The religious tenets learned and practiced in Scotland/Ireland were perpetuated on the frontier. Some of their convictions have been altered or softened over 200 years.

The Associate Reformed Church, a union of two Presbyterian bodies, the Associate Presbyterian Church (Seceders) and the Reformed Presbyterian Church (Covenanters) was formed in America in 1782. As previously noted, some of our early members had already affiliated in Eastern Pennsylvania with the Reformed Church of Dr. John Cuthbertson. The new Associate Reformed Church had a Constitution and Directory of Worship which delineated Church practices.

1. Psalmody—Singing was limited exclusively to the Book of Psalms and did not change at Union Church until 1925, when the Session authorized the use of hymns.

2. Communion—Communion was restricted to church members in good standing. There was no intercommunion with other churches. This applied to both members receiving and ministers offering communion.

3. Baptism—This was a sacrament to be administered only by an ordained minister and in the presence of the Congregation. Godparents were forbidden. In 1838, the Session rebuked the Congregation for not having their children baptized by age 12. That was the rule.

4. Secret Societies—The Church disapproved of Masonry, Odd Fellows, Grange and other organizations whose members pledged secret oaths.

5. Slavery—Involuntary slavery was to be condemned. Slave owners should liberate their slaves and give them their rights as freemen. The practice of buying or selling slaves for gain was condemned. Annual collections to assist in freeing these slaves were held.

6. *Deceased*—They were taken from the house on the day of burial and interred without any ceremony. It has been said that the presence of a minister was unnecessary. At any rate "everything which savors of vain display or fulsome eulogy should be avoided".

7. *Sabbath*—This day was to be kept holy and free from any work or recreation. This restriction applied to religious holidays as well. "Festival days, vulgarly called holy-days, having no warrant in the word of God, are not to be observed." This included Christmas.

8. *Covenanting*—"Public and explicit covenanting with God is a moral duty." It was also noted that United States Churches have never engaged in formal public covenanting as practiced in Scotland.

Do these customs seem quaint to you? Some of our members today can recall the rigidity with which they were practiced. Alice Phillips Davis, a descendant of Jonathan Phillips, remembers stories told about her great, great grandfather, Jonathan. On Sabbath, while riding his horse, he would dismount immediately if he spotted a ball game in progress. The culprits would then be lectured about "keeping the Sabbath holy". Benjamin McCormick recalls his father, Alvin, reminding the family that they were lucky to receive and read the Sunday paper on Saturday evening. Grandfather McCormick forbid reading of the paper on the Sabbath. Ben and Bill McCormick hid their baseball equipment in the barn on Saturdays for a furtive game of "catch" on Sunday. Warren Scott remembered the look of outrage and horror on the faces of his parents when he brought the first deck of cards into their home. Violet Mitchell chuckles as she recalls swinging on a rope in the barn into the hay mow on a Sunday afternoon. Suddenly, her father, Elder Clayton Spear, appeared and admonished Violet and Jean for their boisterous frivolity on the Sabbath.

As the pioneers cleared the land and built their log cabins, they perpetuated old customs, institutions and their language. Prayer and Bible reading were an integral part of family life. Soon families joined together for formal prayer meetings. This was undoubtedly the nucleus of Union Church before formal organization in 1794.

During the Revolutionary War period, this area was engaged in a land struggle between the States of Virginia and Pennsylvania. Each State laid claim to land west of Laurel Ridge and south of the Kiskiminetas, Allegheny and Ohio Rivers. Warrant maps of our immediate area disclose claims were granted by both States to landowners. John Wolff, who was the original owner of Union Church property, had a Virginia certificate as did Benjamin McCormick, John Phillips, Thomas Thornberry and John Bayle, who owned the land purchased by Samuel Scott in 1795. An agreement on boundaries between the two states was reached and ratified by 1786. Washington County was established in 1781 and Allegheny County in 1788.

The Revolutionary War records of most of the veterans buried in Union Cemetery specify service in the "Washington County Militia". Their war was with the Indians, who were fighting for the British and raiding local "plantations", as the farms were called. These raiding parties persisted until 1794.

A favorite site of the Delaware Indians under King Shingas was the mouth of Chartier's Creek, now McKees Rocks. Not too far away was the Mingo trail. To protect themselves the pioneers built forts and block houses. Several were within the vicinity of Union congregation. One of these, known as Fort Cowan was built on the fringe of Settler's Cabin Park. It has been said that it was erected about 1789 by John Peter Bail (Bayle), who owned 400 acres known as "Colebank". The property was later purchased by Samuel and Elizabeth Wilson Scott. During Indian uprisings families lived for days and weeks in these local forts going to work in companies as their crops and stock needed care and protection. They left their families at the fort in care of some trusty guard.

Another fort was located close to Montours Church. When the pioneers were alerted or sensed hostile Indians were lurking about, they stealthily and speedily as possible, took their families to these shelters. An anecdote passed along by pioneer Joseph Scott of Scott's Station recalls Joseph tilling his fields one fine day, and each time he passed a certain cluster of trees his horse balked and fussed. Joseph realized Indians were just beyond the trees, but he continued his work until nearing his cabin. Then, he herded his family together and fled to Montours Fort for safety.

A third fort of some importance was near the mouth of Robinson Run Creek, just west of Carnegie. It was to this sturdy blockhouse, known as Ewing Fort, that the Gabriel and Isaac Walker families retreated in September 1782, after the Indians captured five of their children scalping two of the youngest. The other children were returned in a prisoner of war exchange after the Revolutionary War.

The local forts or blockhouses were sturdy havens of defense. The walls were thick with occasional holes in the chinking for aiming rifles. The floors were earthen. The shape was usually square and double storied with the upper story projecting over the lower about two feet. This enabled defenders to shoot from above any enemy attempting to climb walls. One heavy door opened into the fort. A well-fed spring, water for the occupants, was always nearby.

Compared with European fortresses, the blockhouses seemed crude, but they served the purpose as the Indians had no artillery. Almost all neighborhood forts were built during the 1770's and were frequently used until 1794—the same year Union Church was organized. That summer, General Anthony Wayne defeated the Indian tribes outside the British fort of Fallen Timbers, where Toledo, Ohio is today. This denouement secured the frontier from further Indian uprisings.

Stills were vital to the economy of the pioneers. They learned how to combine excess rye and unlimited spring water into "Monongahela Whiskey", a highly desirable commodity in the East. Whiskey itself became the medium of exchange. It put cash dollars into the pockets of the farmers. How outrageous it appeared to have to pay an Excise Tax on whiskey, the one thing they could trade for needed supplies! To the independent Scotch-Irish, it was government interference at its worst. In 1794, the same year Union was a fledgling church, some of her members were outraged and demonstrated against the tax. This uprising was known as the Whiskey Insurrection or Rebellion. A number of men from this Church were among those who protested having to pay the Excise Tax. They were arrested for their participation. To save the nation from another uprising, ministers were asked to placate their congregations and encourage their members to pay the hated tax. After some persuasion, the local farmers signed a submission to pay, which became known as the "Amnesty." Names from this

Congregation were John Bail, William Hall, John McFadden, Benjamin McCormick, John Nickel, James Thornburg, William Marks, Isaac McMichael, John McMichael, Thomas McMillin, John Phillips, Samuel Scott, Gabriel Walker, Isaac Walker, Joseph Scott, William McCoy and John Porter.

These same men were also great patriots and wholehearted supporters of the American cause during the Revolutionary War. Their names or family names are engraved upon tombstones in our cemetery. There are 24 Revolutionary War Veterans of which we are certain. Perhaps there are more. King George of England referred to this War as a "Presbyterian War", and a Hessian captain called it a "Scotch-Irish Presbyterian Rebellion".

Wherever the Presbyterians settled, a church was soon organized. Then came the schools. Our forefathers were committed to education not only for ministers but for laymen. It was important to be able to read the Bible and Psalter and to participate in the governmental process. Local school boards and private academies in this area were organized and governed by our members. In 1836, Alexander Phillips of this congregation organized a school to teach "reading, writing and arithmetic." The article of agreement lists 17 subscribers. All were members of Union.

From the Session minutes and from minutes of Monongahela Presbytery, we learn that proper behavior was expected from this flock. Lawlessness was forbidden; therefore, the Church acted as an unofficial police force before the existence of the real thing. The Church guided and often governed the life of the pioneer. It provided members with a theological system that was clear, logical and stern. Our Session minutes report that individuals appeared before it for a variety of reasons such as: (1) using profane language in Pittsburgh; (2) slander and falsehood or unbecoming language; (3) intoxication; (4) having been seen in "tippling shops"; (5) selling of liquor to intemperate man; (6) carrying arms on the Sabbath; (7) to avoid a separation or divorce; (8) public dancing and card playing (these folks were suspended indefinitely); (9) for not returning a borrowed shovel; and (10) singing hymns instead of psalms.

FORMAL ORGANIZATION

Previous chapters provided the setting, the people and their religious beliefs. By 1793 or 1794 they were ready for a specific place to worship and to call a pastor. Using the minutes of Monongahela Presbytery, the following material can be documented. It is certain that a "society" or small congregation was organized by September 30, 1793, because a "petition from the united congregations of Robinson Run and Pitts Burgh for a supply of preaching" was heard at a meeting of Monongahela Presbytery. The same request was repeated on October 12, 1793, and Mr. Robert Warwick was appointed to Robinson Run the 3rd Sabbath. On February 6, 1794, Presbytery "heard a verbal petition for a supply of preaching from Robinson Run Congregation by Isaac Walker". Isaac Walker later became one of the first Ruling Elders of Union. The petition was granted and Mr. Matthew Henderson, Jr., was "appointed Sabbath week". Two months later, when Presbytery met at the same place, Robinson's Run asked for a "supply of preaching and the administration of the Sacrament of the Supper". Mr. James McKnight, who was licensed at this same meeting of Presbytery, was "appointed to this service the third Sabbath of April at Robinson Run". It is difficult to tell from Presbytery minutes if "Pittsburgh" referred to Union, although the petition reads "united congregations". However, after "Steep Hollow" and Robinson Run did install Rev. John Riddell as minister of the joint congregations, Presbytery minutes continue to hear petitions from "Pitts-Bourgh" well into 1795 for a supply of preaching. It is doubtful that Union was ever called "Pitts-Bourgh".

At the meeting of Presbytery, held October 20th, 1793, "Mr. Jamieson was appointed to write to Mr. John Riddell of Ireland giving him a fair statement of the great need of faithful ministers of the Gospel in America". Mr. Jamieson probably complied, but it was not necessary, for Mr. Riddell must have been on his way to America at that time. Mr. Riddell was married to Margaret Arnold. Margaret had a brother, John Arnold, who came to the Oakdale area in 1787 with his wife, Margaret Riddell, Rev. John's sister. It appears that Dr. Riddell may have known something about this area before his arrival. At a meeting of Presbytery held May 15, 1794, six and one-half months later, we find this record:

The Rev. John Riddell appeared and produced his credentials, of which the following is a true copy:

ARMAGH, July 2nd. 1793.
The Presbytery of Monaghan being informed that the Rev. John Riddell intends going to America, do hereby testify that he was regularly educated for the holy ministry, that he received a Degree of Master of Arts at the University of Glasgow, that he is an ordained minister of the Gospel, free of publick scandal or ground of church censure known to us, and that he may be received by any congregation or Presbytery where God in his Providence orders his lot, being in full communion with the Presbytery of Monaghan at his departure.
     Andrew Caldwell, Mod'r.
     John Rodgers, Cl'k, pro tem.

N.B. He is married to Margaret Arnold who is also a regular member and I do also certify that frequent Applications were made to our Presbytery from America for preachers, and the Associate Synod of Ireland ordered their Presbyteries to give a bene dicissit to any preacher who chooses to go.
     John Rodgers, clerk of Associate Synod

You will notice that his "credentials" bear a date three and one half months before Mr. Jamieson was directed to write. Presbytery accepted his recommendation, added his name to the roll of Presbytery and "invited him to a seat, which he accordingly took." At this same meeting we find that Presbytery received a petition from the "united congregations of Robinson's Run and Steep Hollow," praying Presbytery to settle the Rev. John Riddell among them as their pastor, with all possible expedition." The petition was "sustained as a Gospel call", presented to the candidate and by him accepted. Presbytery met a month later and appointed the Sacrament of the Supper to be administered at Robinson's Run, the third Sabbath of August, and then adjourned "to meet at Robinson's Run tent" on the 15th of August, for the installation of Mr. Riddell, Mr. Matthew Henderson, Jr. to preside and Mr. Jamieson to assist.

The following is a quote from Presbytery minutes of August 15, 1794:

> Appointed a messenger to go immediately to the Tent and read a certification to the people of this congregation now assembled, that the Presbytery is now constituted, and as Mr. Riddell's Edict has been formerly served, if any person, or persons, have objections to his installment to come forward and show reason why Presbytery should not proceed, or otherwise, his installment will take place immediately after the forenoon sermon. No person appearing to object, Presbytery proceeded to the Tent, and after a sermon by Mr. Henderson from I. Peter v: 2, 'Feed the flock of God.' the congregation signified their continued adherence to the call. Mr. Riddell was called forward, answered the usual questions, and was by supplication and prayer, set apart to the pastoral charge of the united congregations of Robinson's Run and Steep Hollow.

From the above references to "Steep Hollow", it is clear that Robinson Run and Steep Hollow Congregations were inextricably joined at Presbytery level and with a shared ministry.

With Mr. Riddell shepherding both flocks, the congregations grew. The first statistical tables recorded in Presbytery minutes are dated 1804, ten years after Mr. Riddell's arrival. This report gives "125 families" and "260 adults" for the two congregations. Supposing them to be of equal strength, we have 62 families belonging to Union. In 1814 he reported 410 members, and in 1815, 429 members. These were the largest congregations in Monongahela Presbytery at that time.

Both congregations prospered, so it is not surprising to find in Presbytery minutes on September 11, 1816, at a meeting in Robinson's Run, that Mr. Riddell applied for the dissolution of the pastoral relation between himself and the "Lower Branch" of his charge. (Sometime previous to this year, Steep Hollow came to be known as "Lower Robinson's Run", or "Lower Branch"). Mr. Riddell's reason was stated as follows: "As each branch of my congregation has made arrangements whereby they will be enabled to enjoy the entire labors of a stated pastor

—to prepare the way for so desirable an event, I hereby request the Presbytery to release me from the pastoral charge of the Lower Branch of my congregation." Signed, John Riddell. Presbytery's record furnishes the following: "Agreeably to a contract recently entered into betwixt both parts of the congregation, the Lower Branch consented to relinquish their claim to Mr. Riddell's labors."

Finally, after being referred to as "Lower Robinson's Run", "Lower Branch", "Steep Hollow", we received our identity! On November 6, 1816 at Presbytery meeting, "The Congregation from which Mr. Riddell was released having taken the name of Union desire to be known by that name on the records of Presbytery. They also petitioned for a supply of sermon and the moderation of a call. Mr. Riddell was appointed to moderate the call."

The second minister, Mr. Moses Kerr, who also emigrated from Ireland, was called and "offered the sum of $550.00 annually to be increased to $600.00 when seats in their church are fully occupied." Monongahela Presbytery minutes record that Rev. Kerr was asked specifically about "the resolution proffered by Presbytery in June 1816, to present difficulties on the subject of intercommunion." They wanted to know whether Rev. Kerr "was willing to acquiesce therein. . . . He declared himself satisfied therewith. After which the call was presented to him which he accepted." Rev. Kerr was installed the first Wednesday of May 1819, at a Presbytery meeting held at Union. This Presbytery resolution forbid Associate Reformed ministers to administer communion to members of other churches. We do not know if Rev. Kerr was able to fill the pews, but the last clause in his call regarding an "increase" appears to have caused a problem with the pastor and the congregation. Presbytery was called upon several times to adjust financial difficulties between them. In support of Mr. Kerr, 86 members of the congregation signed the following petition:

> 1st. We applied to him to relinquish his petition for disconnection, and continue his pastoral labors among us.
>
> 2nd. His removal will essentially injure the congregation, for some have already applied to other congregations, and a number of others will as soon as they know Mr. Kerr will be released.

3rd. His unremitting care to serve our interests since his settlement among us, the obligations we came under when we called him to be our pastor binds us to our fidelity in our duty to him.

4th. Many of his hearers will advance their stipends considerably; young persons and others who did not belong to Church have desired to contribute for his continuance with us.

5th. Neutrals will support Mr. Kerr as long as he is their minister.

6th. In case of his removal many of the aged despair of ever again seeing a fixed pastor, and the young anticipate with grief the loss of his service.

These are the oldest papers of any description relating to congregations to be found. Whether they are on record or not we cannot say. Mr. Kerr was released from the pastorate about one year after this, November, 1827." Controversy over salary due Mr. Kerr continued through 1829. At Presbytery meeting on June 24, 1829, Mr. Kerr applied for the interference of Presbytery to urge Union Congregation to settle with him. In compliance with his request it was moved "that notice be given to said congregation that unless they settle and discharge the balance of salary due to Mr. Kerr before next meeting of Presbytery, they will receive no further supply of sermon." This motion was adopted and the clerk was directed to transmit a copy of the resolution to the trustees of Union Church.

Another petition was presented to Presbytery from the congregation October 2, 1832, for the moderation of a call for Andrew S. Fulton. Mr. Fulton was installed as pastor on May 28, 1833 at a salary of $500.00. Mr. Fulton in petitioning for his release from the congregation in August 13, 1839, penned a revealing report. "I have long felt that the burden of so large a congregation was too heavy for me, placed within reach of one hundred and fifty families, bound to attend to their various calls and in the country, too, when it is not possible to make more than four to five calls in the day. Charged with much session business and with the labours of the pulpit on ordinary and extraordinary occasions and then called off one fifth of the time upon foreign business, servicing vacant congregations or attending to the concerns of the Church at large. I have all along felt that this imposed more labour upon the body, and more cares and vexations upon the mind than almost any one man should attempt to perform. Within the last two years my labours have increased in rapid proportion, and I have surrendered myself up to them with a greater devotedness than ever. Had it not been for a harmony remarkable for so large a congregation, with which providence has sincerely blessed us, I never could have got along as well as I have done. It is my pride, and my honor to say that I have been supported by a session the most agreeable I ever met with, and that my reliance upon the attachment of the congregation has cheered me on through all difficulties and encouraged me to attempt what I should otherwise have considered impossible."

Mr. Fulton continues with revelations regarding his poor health and refers to his brethern in the ministry who were "called from this earthly scene." Apparently, other things were on his mind, too. As his petition goes on, he addresses a contentious problem. He has delayed his decision to leave "had Providence not furnished an opportunity, which I was far from seeking and to which I allude with sincere sorrow. I refer to the last meeting when I was with you, and when the question of abolishing lining was before you. (Lining refers to "lining" out the Psalms for singing.) You will remember that the decision went against my wishes. But just after I had arisen and expressed my cordial submission to the will of the majority and warmly and affectionately exhorted all others to do the same, just as I had done for months previous, when the question was likewise before you, I was suddenly subjected to a storm of abusive language such I believe as I never received from my childhood until that day. This treatment of myself together with what was suffered by others on that day and which was equally gross, has left such a strong impression on my feelings that it is my sincere belief that I can never be happy in laboring here. I acknowledge with pleasure that no member of the congregation in good and regular standing is chargeable with participating in this conduct. Still, however, I cannot continue as heretofore to labour among you without a loss of self-respect and without a constant apprehension for similar treatment whenever my duty would call me to say or do to any person what might not be pleasant either to them or myself as a pastor must often do. Accordingly, it is my unalterable action (I say so with all affectionate respect), to prosecute a separation. I say unalterable, to prevent any kind and partial friends from indulging hope which must be disappointed. Signed Andrew S. Fulton"

This petition as copied in Monongahela Presbytery Minutes, gives us splendid insights into our Church in 1839. This missive is before we had any written records of our own. First, we know the congregation was "large", with 150 families and spread out and that travel was difficult. Outreach was successful because he alludes that matters must have been going well, for he refers to the "harmony" in the large congregation in addition to complimenting the Session. However, we learn that the subject of "lining" was offensive to some members of "questionable" standing in Union Church. (To learn more about the controversial "lining", the reader is advised to see "music".) It appears that the behavior of some members toward Mr. Fulton caused his resignation.

Present church, circa 1938.

2
Land and Buildings

The newly formed Congregation of Union not only sought a supply of preaching from Monongahela Presbytery in 1793, they also sought a permanent place to worship and build their Church. In an Allegheny County court document dated June 20, 1834, John McMichael, an early member and an elder, testified that forty years previously, "Union Congregation employed me to purchase of John Wolf five acres of land for the purpose of erecting a house for public worship". He made the purchase from John Wolf of five acres of land and paid him ten pounds for the property. The Congregation refunded John McMichael. The deposition continues, "Shortly after the purchase of said five acres of land from said Wolf the late Hugh McCurdy purchased the balance of the tract of land of Wolf . . . About the year 1795 or '96, the Congregation erected a meeting house on said land and has ever since continued to occupy it as a place of public worship. Some time before the erection of a meeting house the Rev. John Riddell accepted of a call from said Congregation and continued to officiate as their pastor until about the year 1816".

John Wolf, the original owner, purchased approximately 350 acres, which he named "Limestone", on a Virginia certificate in 1791. He did not keep his property long, for after selling Union Church five acres in 1794, he sold the remainder to Hugh McCurdy in 1795.

Four subsequent purchases were made in the 1800's and four more parcels of land were added in the first half of this century. From the combined property purchases, the Church and Cemetery together own about 25 acres. The five acres purchased from Wolf are part of the Cemetery.

Andrew McFarland and Mary, his wife, deeded to the Congregation of Union forever on August 14, 1834, 99 perches for the sum of $40.00. This is the part on which the church building now stands. Benjamin K. Palmer and Sara, his wife, deeded to Union Congregation 84.4 perches for the sum of $74.20 on February 22, 1847. This is the part on which the old sheds to house horses and carriages once stood. Besides this, the church owned 5 acres and 110 perches adjoining the south side of the church property. There was once a parsonage on this site. This was purchased by the Congregation for the sum of $3,900.00. The coal beneath the property was sold for $1,179.20 and the property later sold for $10,000.00.

After completion of the present church, the ground seemed to be inadequate, and so 66 perches on the west side were donated by John Palmer.

In 1925, a lot adjoining the church property and fronting on the Steubenville Pike was purchased from Henry and Julia Astfalk for the sum of $1,000. On this lot a parsonage and garage were erected.

In 1952, two additional parcels totaling 4 acres were added. These were purchased from Joseph D. McCurdy and Eva, his wife, and from Amy Florence Heckle. It is anticipated that this ground will be part of the Cemetery.

How thrilled the young congregation of Union must have been when they acquired their first property. The author of Union's first history says, "Like Abraham of old these early settlers, wherever and whenever they pitched their tents, they built their altar. The first church or house of worship for this congregation was a tent of poles some 8 x 10 feet." Our perception of a "tent" is something canvas, but this was not so in 1794. Tents then were a rustic shelter covered with boughs to shelter the preacher and his Bible. A high stump or slab log fastened between two trees became the pulpit. Hillsides which ran up or down served as a natural amphitheater for these crude wooden shelters. The site of our first church, somewhere in the center of the old cemetery was a perfect location.

The first "church" or building, was probably erected around 1794 or '95, according to John McMichael's court deposition. It "was a log cabin, a hollow square, with eight corners resembling a Greek cross in shape. The front and rear arms were ten feet square; the others twenty feet square, making an audience chamber 20 x 50 feet. This church building was furnished with a pulpit in the rear arm; this pulpit was some eight feet high, with steps for entering leading from the floor on either side. In front of this pulpit there was a choir stand some four feet high; this stand only accommodated two persons, one to line out the Psalm, the other to pitch the tune. This church was at first seated with puncheons, afterwards with modern pews. This was built in the fall of 1794. It was located down in the old grave-yard, near where McFarland's monument now stands."

The next church building, constructed in 1832, was a simple structure built of brick and located on the present site. This building was partly demolished by a storm December 9, 1855. Fortunately, because of the storm, no preaching was held that Sabbath, for had there been, the pastor and many others would have been killed or injured in the wreckage that covered the pulpit and the front rows of pews. In 1847, the corporation minutes show that a house was built for the sexton.

While the third church was being erected in 1856, the congregation met in a local schoolhouse (probably Hall School on DeVassie Road). It was constructed of brick and consisted of a vestibule and session room, a large auditorium and a small room above the vestibule where the infant class met. This building was heated with coal stoves. The trustees required in 1867, that fires be put on 2 hours previous to the service and kept up so that the building would not fall below 75 degrees. A fire was to be kept in the session room to accommodate nursing women. When new stoves had to be purchased in 1874, the trustees simply asked for more "pew money." Stables for the horses which brought members to church were constructed in 1865. A parsonage and lot were purchased from Hugh Brown in 1876, for $3,900.00. It was located across Church Road in the area of the shopping center. The third church building was razed in 1899 to give place to our present structure of buff brick, which was dedicated June 9, 1901.

At a congregational meeting held March 2, 1899, it was decided to build a new church. The building, one story in height, of Pompeian brick with stone trimming, provided an auditorium to seat 400 people and a Sabbath School auditorium with separate classrooms. The new building was completed in 1901 and dedicated free of debt at a total cost of $29,886.99, plus material from the old building. Of this sum $12,869.74 was received from the sale of oil on the church property; $16,017.25 was raised by subscriptions of the members.

In 1925, a new parsonage was built at the foot of the hill consisting of seven rooms, a bath and reception hall, and a finished third floor. This building of red brick with stone trimmings is well constructed and gracious. Our pastors have not resided in the parsonage since 1968. The trustees rent this home as commercial property.

In 1924, the church was re-decorated and the art glass windows repaired at a cost of $4,980.10. Another refurbishing program was undertaken in 1939. At this time, the roof was repaired, a new heating plant was installed, the interior was redecorated, the exterior trim was painted and the organ cleaned.

After World War II, the congregation grew in leaps and bounds. Returning veterans married the girl back home. This ushered in a "baby boom". More space was needed for the little ones and for increased activities—social and religious. The Session authorized a building program to be known as "Another Crossroads". A quote from the campaign brochure reads, "Since the war our numbers have doubled, from 280 to 560. Our sanctuary is filled to overflowing each Sabbath morning. Our Bible School attendance is running 60% ahead of one year ago! Our kitchen and dining room facilities are inadequate for maintaining an attractive, growing social program."

We were fortunate to have an architect in the Church, W. Stuart Forsythe, who drew the plans for modernization and expansion. The sanctuary seating capacity was enlarged by one-third through installation of a folding partition behind the chancel to open into the Bible School. The Bible School capacity was doubled by remodeling the basement and making further excavation. At that time the portion of the basement under the sanctuary was unexcavated. The previous basement consisted of the portion under the circular Sabbath School.

The kitchen was enlarged and modernized. A church office and study were converted from existing space on the first floor. Later, this study became a "Bride's Room." A new system for heating the entire building was installed. The parking area was doubled in capacity and the driveway was paved completely.

The cost of this entire program was $50,000. At this time, 1954, our total budget was $18,592. Dr. William F. Ruschhaupt, Jr., who had been with us since 1946, was our pastor.

Shortly after Rev. Cook's installation at Union, the pulpit was recarpeted and new chairs and a lectern replaced the old ones. These refurbishings were made possible by Mr. and Mrs. J. A. Scott and Mr. and Mrs. S. H.Scott.

In 1954, during the tenure of Dr. Ruschhaupt the congregation erected the first of three crosses atop the steeple. Union Church sits on one of the highest points in Allegheny County, so the cross was visible for many miles. This first cross was made of white plastic and was erected using a crane furnished by Phillips Contracting Company. It blew down during a violent wind storm. The cross was soon replaced with one made of red plastic. It was shattered by lightening. Not to be rebuffed by the forces of nature, a third cross was elevated. The present white cross is made of wood and laminated with stainless steel. It is topped with a lightening rod. A helicopter installed the cross and it is emplaced over a twelve inch pin.

The beautiful Church on the hill was busily engaged in God's work and the Lord had looked favorably upon us. It was now 1965, and we needed more room for our Christian Education Program. Plans for the new Educational wing were drawn by W. Stuart Forsythe and presented to the Congregation. The addition was completed in 1968, at a cost of $319,000. A legacy of $40,000 from the Emma Reed Estate helped defray costs. William C. Cook was the pastor. The mortgage for this building campaign was burned at a special ceremony on February 14, 1973.

Deep currents of discontent were rife in the Church in 1974. After the problem was resolved in 1975, (you will read more about this in another chapter), our spirits were lifted. Members were imbued with that indomitable spirit which typifies Presbyterians. Resolving to carry on, it was decided that our Sanctuary should be remodeled and repainted. Led by the Holy Spirit and with some professional help, the men of the Church did all the work under the direction of Elder Jack Howard. The floor of the sanctuary was raised and adjusted to accommodate new horizontal pews instead of the former curved oak pews. The overflow room (former Sunday School) was incorporated into part of the sanctuary with installation of pews. In the choir loft, the organ was moved from the center to the side, enabling the organist to see the minister and the congregation. The kitchen also received refurbishing.

This experience of working together fulfilled a spiritual and emotional need. The Lord spoke to us. He brought our congregation together through working toward a common goal and through fellowship and prayer.

In 1984, a ramp to accommodate the handicapped was constructed. It leads into the right front door of the Sanctuary. This improvement was funded by the Joseph McCurdy estate. The following year, 1985, a Memorial Garden was designed by Glenn Uffelman and built between the two front entrances. Urns and benches dedicated to the memory of loved ones were grouped aesthetically in the garden. They are planted with flowers each Spring and enhance the appearance of the main entrance.

At this writing there is talk of further remodeling. We don't know where or when, but it is sure to come, just as it has in the past. Whatever we have done, it has always been for the glory of the Lord.

Union Presbyterian ladies group, circa 1917.

3
Church Officers

ELDERS

Without written records it is difficult to ascertain much about the Church officers as early as 1794. From Presbytery records and from the first Church histories, we know that there were at least four elders in 1794: Isaac Walker, William Marks, Sr., Jonathan Phillips and Isaac McMichael. The latter was not mentioned in the first history, but his name appears in minutes of Monongahela Presbytery as attending meetings from 1774 through 1822. All of these men are buried in Union Cemetery.

The session minutes of February 20, 1835, list six members: Alexander Phillips, Samuel Glass, Sr., William Hall, William Watt, George McKee and John McMichael. There were increases and decreases in the number of men serving on the Session. The highest number was in 1959, when there were 15. After the upheaval in 1975, the session was reduced to 12 members where it remains today.

For over 150 years Union's elders were elected for a lifetime of active service. Unless an elder resigned or died, there was no change in its composition. It was not until 1958 that a rotation system began. There were terms of three years, with the option of serving a second term of three. Another milestone was reached in 1980, when our first woman elder was elected, Jacqueline Pfaub. Elders who have served from 1794 through 1993 are registered in Appendix E.

In the early years the Session met three times a year. The meeting lasted for two days. By the end of the 19th century they were meeting more frequently. In 1897, they voted to hold one meeting per month.

The function of the Session in early days was to examine members to determine worthiness for membership and for communion. This body policed their flock. They acted as a court to arbitrate quarrels among communicants. They meted out justice in cases of breach of marriage, fraud, blasphemy, violation of the Sabbath, slander, public dancing, card playing, singing hymns (instead of Psalms), card playing and other offenses which we consider trivial today.

We may smile and think this quaint, but as we reflect on the untamed frontier of Western Pennsylvania in the 19th century, these United Presbyterians fulfilled a vital function. They demanded exemplary behavior from their members by threatening to withhold communion or by "sessioning" them. This meant the offender must appear before the session and acknowledge guilt and say he was sorry. He would then be restored to former standing and privileges of the church.

Serving Communion to worthy members was an important function of the elders, just as it is today. In early years it was celebrated once or twice a year and lasted several days. Wednesday or Thursday preceding Sabbath was generally a day of fasting and prayer. Saturday was a day of preparation when a sermon was delivered on the meaning of the sacrament. Sometime during this period members were visited and examined by a member of the Session or the preacher to determine worthiness to partake of the elements. If a member was deemed properly prepared to receive the sacrament, a small token was given. These communion "tokens" were small pieces of lead or leather with a distinctive identifying letter or symbol to designate the church.

Communion day, on the Sabbath, lasted seven to nine hours. It began with singing of the Psalms led by a gentleman called a "precentor", standing in front of the pulpit. This was followed by a long sermon, then a discourse on the Sacraments. The long tables in the front were then "fenced" as the preacher enumerated all sins in the decalogue plus others. The object was self-examination and repentance. The minister then invited participants to come forward. An elder at each table collected the "token", for no one received communion without having received this symbol of preparedness. Bread and wine were offered. The wine was in a common cup and passed along the table. We can only imagine that a napkin was used to wipe the cup as it made its way along. Fermented wine was used until 1884, when grape juice was served.

Communicants returned to their pews after receiving the elements and another group proceeded to the table. At each seating the minister delivered an address to those at the table. After all were served a final exhortation was delivered. If you concluded the service was long, it was indeed!

An intermission followed the exhortation. This provided an opportunity for visitation, lunch, discreet courting, recipe and fashion exchange. How they must have looked forward to this great event! Contact with the outside world was limited in this vast and undeveloped countryside.

An afternoon sermon several hours long followed. It was permissible to move about or go to sleep for the day was long and some had traveled many miles.

The entire event culminated on Monday after the thanksgiving meditation and benediction. Imagine this type of service today! We cannot question the spiritual depth of our forbears.

Through the years, adjustments were made regarding communion. In 1893, the Session permitted "outside" church-goers having asked permission, to commune with us. In 1897, if members of other churches were in attendance at our communion service, they were invited to participate. Previous to this, the Associate Reformed/ United Presbyterian Church practiced "closed communion".

In 1894, communion tables were no longer used and it was agreed to dispose of the table linen used on them. Proceeds were to be allocated to the Session fund. A set of individual communion cups was presented in 1904, and individual cup receivers were placed on the back of the pews. A new communion service was purchased in 1920 and the old one was repaired and presented to our own missionaries, Rev. and Mrs. Willard Acheson, for use in the Foreign Mission Field. From the 1946 Church history we read:

> A silver communion cup, which was used at the first communion service held in April 1794, in the Robinson Run district, is in the possession of the congregation. This cup was presented to the congregation June 9, 1901, by G. H. Moore of Pittsburgh as a memorial to Mrs. Ann Jane Moore.

Gradually communion services were increased from one per year to three in the latter part of the 19th century. In 1917, it was voted to celebrate four times per year and in 1993, we will hold monthly Communion services.

DEACONS

The Board of Deacons serves the Church in so many ways. They decorate the Sanctuary for Christmas and Easter. They deliver the pulpit flowers to the shut-ins, and maintain a greeting card supply corner. They prepare, set-up and clean-up communion elements. They collect and maintain a food cupboard and provide food certificates for those experiencing difficulties, and they direct parking of cars for special occasions.

The first Board of Deacons was established at a Congregational meeting on June 9, 1894, when five men were elected. This Board apparently disbanded shortly after that date, for there are no existing records. They are not noted in the Church history in 1944. In January 1955, they reorganized with eight men serving. At their first meeting, they established a "Deacon's Fund" to help the needy. The officers elected in 1955 were: Wilson Tidball, President, Otto Persons, Vice

Christian Education building addition, completed 1968.

President and Sam Mitchell, Secretary/Treasurer. Our first women deacons, Helen Brammer and Anna Phillips, were elected in 1966. At present, there are 15 members on that Board. A list of deacons who have served over the years is recorded in Appendix E.

TRUSTEES

The finances of Union Congregation have always been under a board of trustees. The first board members of which we have any record were George McKee, Sr., Jonathan Phillips and John Hall. These men were elected sometime previous to August 26, 1811. The next board of which we have any mention was elected previous to 1834, when they signed a deposition in Allegheny County Court regarding Church property. They were: David McKee, William Hall, Hugh McCormick and William Gribbon. The Charter, written in 1847 provided for three trustees. This was amended in 1907, to provide for six. At the present time there are six serving on that board.

All Church property and deeds are held in the name of trustees representing "Associate Reformed Congregation for Robinson Township" and that denomination only. Of course, we have since had three mergers within the Presbyterian Church. Therefore, the land is held for "The Presbyterian Church U.S.A."

The Church Charter of 1847 delineates the duties of the trustees as collecting pew rents, keeping an account and giving the money to the treasurer of the Corporation.

In the early days there were no pews, but benches were used to seat the congregation. When better church structures were built, the church was partly supported by the money received from pew sales and rentals. The position of the pew within the sanctuary was an important consideration. Choice seats were near the front of the church.

Occasionally, the pew revenues failed to provide adequate support for the church. In frequent cases, the church had difficulty in collecting pew rents. When money was short, they simply raised the pew rent. In 1846, session minutes reveal some strong discussion over the legitimacy of this practice. The gentleman protesting claimed, "he would be a thorn in the flesh and he would keep his pew" refusing to pay the higher cost. Soon after that, Corporation minutes state that "any member of the Congregation neglecting to pay his stipend within 90 days will be turned over to an officer for collection." Pew holders were required to pay stipends semi-annually in March and September. In 1852, the Trustees levied $50.00 on pews to be collected with the stipends already on the pews. Ten years later they raised the prices again by 50%.

The system failed to carry out the principle of proportionate giving. The seats were rented at different prices but the amount charged was not commensurate with the financial ability of the individual. The poor widow was unable to attend unless she would take a free seat reserved for the poor. The person who gave the most amounts was awarded the choice seat. This system created a class consciousness.

Another objection to the pew system was that it discouraged visitors and new people from attending services. In the pew rent system, one was expected to rent a pew before he would be allowed to hear the Word. Pew rents were abolished at Union in 1876, in favor of voluntary contributions. A pew rental chart from 1856, is framed and on display. Accompanying records from the trustee minutes spell out the rules, "Any person purchasing a pew will be required to pay the purchase money within sixty days from this date (October 13, 1856). No pew holder will be permitted to put any shelf or other obstruction under his pew except it be to close under in front."

The envelope system was adopted in 1878-79, and in 1880, pledging was authorized. The Trustees presented a printed message along with appropriate cards to the members urging them to subscribe and place their contributions weekly in the basket as it is presented on Sabbath day. An interesting comment in bold face type at the end of their message reads: "PERSONS ATTENDING THIS CHURCH WHO ARE UNPROVIDED WITH PEWS OR SITTINGS, CAN SECURE THEM BY APPLICATION TO THE TRUSTEES".

Union's trustees have been diligent in the upkeep and beautification of our building. They have never allowed it to deteriorate inside or outside. They have provided the impetus for all the remodelings and additions over the years. Names of the trustees elected from 1811 through 1992 are listed in Appendix E.

Sabbath (Sunday) school room—1944.

Church sanctuary—1944.

4
Activities and Organizations

SABBATH SCHOOL/SUNDAY SCHOOL

Records show that in the year 1845 Dr. Ekin, who was at that time pastor of Union Church, undertook to form a Sabbath School in the congregation. Opposition ran so high that he was denied the use of the church, and after some three or four meetings at the sexton's house, they had to abandon the undertaking. So you see it was not altogether smooth sailing for those members who wished to keep abreast of the times. Though these were only some of the failures, it must not be taken for granted that all new enterprises shared the same fate, not by any means. So it was not until June 11, 1859, that a Sabbath School was permanently organized by a few of the bolder members of the congregation. There were about fifty persons enrolled in this first Sabbath School, these divided into eight classes.

At first there were many difficulties to overcome. One of the greatest being that at this time the congregation was without a pastor and there was no one well versed in the manners and methods of conducting a Sabbath School, to assist and encourage. Some of the most influential members of the church and of the community were opposed to this sort of teaching. For a good many years there were no lesson helps of any kind, so officers and teachers had to rely on their own judgment and ability to instruct their classes. According to the earliest memories we can find, the lessons consisted mostly of answering questions from the Catechism and repeating Bible verses which had been memorized. The aim of the leaders at all times being to overcome all opposition, gain the good will of those who attended, and in time draw over those who were opposed to the principles of Sabbath School instruction. This was no easy task and required both time and patience. How well these early leaders succeeded in their undertaking may be judged by the record of great things accomplished through the years.

Two years after the organization, a library was purchased. This put new life into the undertaking, for books were not very plentiful in those days. A great many more children began to attend that they might have access to those books. With the increased attendance, interest in the Sabbath School grew. Officers and teachers were encouraged to go on. In less than ten years from the time of its organization, the Sabbath School of Union Church had every member on its side.

There have been many changes since those first ten hard years. Lesson helps of various kinds have been provided. Graded lessons were introduced so that now there are little leaflets suitable for the tiny Beginners, interesting work for Intermediate and Junior groups, and Quarterlies with dependable helps and commentaries for the Adults. For the many years that we have had our present church building, there have been separate class rooms for each class. The library is still carried on, though its popularity has decreased with the increased supply of books and magazines in the homes.

For two years beginning in January 1917, a twelve month course in Teachers Training was carried on. The book "Preparation for Teaching," by Rev. Charles Oliver was used for text. In the two classes twenty-four persons completed their training. A great many of these have made use of their training by teaching classes at Union and elsewhere. The number enrolled in the Sabbath School has varied greatly from time to time. The 1944 enrollment was two hundred and forty-three, with thirteen classes. For a number of years the Primary and Intermediate groups met under the guidance of a Junior Superintendent in the regular Sabbath School room, for opening exercises. The Juniors and the Adults gather in the auditorium for their opening services. The Sabbath School contributions were used to purchase supplies, the remainder goes to the missions.

With the exception of the annual Sabbath School picnic and the Sabbath School Convention, to which we sent delegates, all the social activities are sponsored by the different organized classes. The School as a group sent Christmas packages to our Service personnel.

At the present time, 1993, the Sabbath School activity is called Sunday School. Some adult classes gather in the sanctuary for opening exercises. The current studies are taken from prepared quarterly lessons, however, there are some classes who simply study directly from the Bible. There are currently about 55 adults and 80 children members who regularly attend Sunday School. Altogether, there are 8 classes. The adult giving is given to the current church fund because the supplies are purchased through this account. The children's offering is given to a deserving mission activity.

A short individual history of the many Sunday School classes follows. However, it is important to note that many classes have come and gone throughout the years.

WOMEN'S BIBLE CLASS

This class, composed of the more elderly women of the congregation, was one of the most faithful groups in the Sabbath School. Their record shows a high percentage of attendance each Sabbath and a liberal offering. Through the years they have done what they could to relieve need and help in the upkeep of the church. They set an example to all in their quiet, unassuming Christian lives. Never formally organized they worked as a class group for years. In 1944, there were ten members. This class ceased after 1944.

MINISTERS CLASS

The men of the congregation became an organized class October, 25, 1926. They adopted the name "Friendship Class" and chose the motto "Go get 'em." Later around 1944 it became known as the "Men's Adult Bible Class" or the "Ministers Class," since the minister had always been its teacher. The Class maintained its own treasury and contributed to various worthy causes. We found those men to be a bulwark of strength and assurance at all times. This class also ceased after 1944.

LOYAL DAUGHTERS

This class of women, recognizing the benefit to be derived from being organized, became a member of the O.A.B.C. on February 7th, 1913, with twenty-four members. The class name "Loyal Daughters" was chosen and the motto "We are in the King's Business."

The class maintained its own treasury through funds derived from annual dues of members, the diversion of a stated amount from the weekly collections and the proceeds from the various class enterprises. This class always aided in the financing of improvements to church and parsonage. They helped substantially in carrying out the "Five Year Plan" of improving and beautifying the church.

Many worthwhile organizations such as Missions, Colleges and The Salvation Army received donations.

During World War I, the class supported the young daughter of a deceased French soldier. During World War II, they contributed to the Red Cross, sponsored a drive for needed equipment for the Deshon Hospital for wounded Veterans, and have sent "The Upper Room" to each service man and woman from our own church. Each year they made scrapbooks for some Children's or Soldiers Hospital and made their President a life member of the W.G.M.S.

This class was instrumental in organizing the Home Department. It no longer exists today.

WILLING WORKERS

During April of 1914, the Willing Workers' Bible Class organized with thirteen charter members. These members became scattered and an almost entirely new group reorganized in November 1919 with almost twice their original membership.

The class supported the program of the United Presbyterian Church. Funds for the treasury are kept up by class dues, a percentage of each Sabbath's collection and the proceeds derived from class enterprises. They have done what they could to relieve need in the community in several instances, have always helped to finance church improvements and donated a substantial sum to help carry out the "Five Year Plan." Their principal missionary endeavor is the sending of $60.00 annually to our Mission Field in Egypt and the $25.00 of Thank-offering with which they made their president a life member of the W.G.M.S. They have done knitting and sewing for the Red Cross, and sent packages to our men and women in the service. They contributed to the support of a British child. Each Christmas they sent sunshine baskets to the shut-ins of the church. One member is still living in a nursing home and the group is no longer active.

THE YOUNG MEN'S CLASS

The Young Men's Bible Class was organized in 1927 with a membership of thirty-five. These young men did their part in the work of the church, serving as ushers, assistant superintendent or teachers. At different times they have provided funds and clothing to the needy. When the new parsonage was built, this class purchased shrubbery for the lawn. For a time they paid for a scholarship for a young man in Egypt under the supervision of Dr. Willard Acheson, our missionary there. More than any other class, this one was drained of its membership by World War II, both into the armed forces and into the defense work. Their aim always was the advancement of Christ's Kingdom. This class is no longer active.

FOR OTHERS BIBLE CLASS

The For Others Bible Class was organized in the summer of 1918 with twenty charter members. Through the years contributions have been made to various worthy causes such as Near East Relief, New World Movement and the support and education of an Egyptian girl in one of our mission schools.

The class has always helped in any church improvements and they donated liberally to the "Five Year Plan." They have done knitting for the Red Cross and sponsored a drive for a contribution to the local Red Cross Unit. They sent packages to Union's service personnel. The group is relatively inactive, but up to 1992 they maintained a checking account and they supplied flowers for the pulpit in memory of their most recent friends who have gone to be with the Lord. At present, this class still exists, but the members are few.

FAITHFUL HELPERS

The Faithful Helper's Sabbath School Class was organized in 1926 with fifteen members. The class motto was "If at first you don't succeed, try, try again." In 1929, they gave a lovely Easter Pageant, with the help of some others. They have done sewing for the New Covenant Mission of Pittsburgh. In May 1929, the class was united with another group which had been organized under the name "Persevering Helpers."

A new organization was made, and the name, "Faithful Helpers" retained. This class made a contribution to the "Five Year Plan," knitted afghans for the Red Cross and at different times have made dolls and scrapbooks for Childrens Hospitals. This class has ceased since 1944.

PERSEVERING HELPERS BIBLE CLASS

The Persevering Helpers Class was organized May 7, 1927, with fifteen charter members. They had a Devotional Committee, one member of which took charge of class devotions for each month. The dues were ten cents a month. They contributed five dollars to Thank-Offering in 1929 and three dollars for the purchase of books for the Sabbath School library. This class combined with the Faithful Helpers class in 1929.

ALWAYS FAITHFUL CLASS

This class, composed of the teenage girls of the Sabbath School, was organized May 16th, 1942. They selected the name "ALWAYS FAITHFUL." They had many social gatherings but did not attend regular class meetings. The same group made up the Junior Girls choir. They have knitted patches for Red Cross ambulance robes. In the short period of their organization they made a very important place for themselves in the church. This class does not exist any more.

HOME DEPARTMENT

During the Reverend H. C. Hildebrand's pastorate, the need of a Home Department in our Sabbath School was recognized. Chiefly through the instrumentality of the Loyal Daughters Bible Class, this organization was made. Literature was provided for the members, who consist of persons not able to get out to church services. This class no longer exists.

CRADLE ROLL

During the Reverend J. M. Briceland's pastorate a committee was appointed to organize a Cradle Roll. All the children of the church under four years of age are enrolled. At the time of the 1944 writing, on Children's Day each child was remembered with a flower. Today, Cathleen Scott maintains the Cradle Roll. Each newborn receives a

Cradle Roll certificate signed by the pastor welcoming the child into the church. A packet of helpful information on parenting and the importance of nurturing the child in a Christian home is presented to parents. Bi-monthly newsletters on the same topics are mailed. The Cradle Roll sends a birthday card to the child on his first birthday and on the second he is promoted to the Nursery Department of the Sunday School. At birth each baby is recognized by a red rose on the altar, and an announcement card is placed on a special Cradle Roll bulletin board.

WOMEN'S MISSIONARY SOCIETY

At the time of the organization of this congregation and for many years afterward, women were not expected to take an active part in the work of the church and we have no record of any organization for Christian work among the women until the Women's Missionary Society was organized February 23, 1880. Since that time the work has been faithfully carried forward. "Never very many in numbers, but always with a steadfast purpose overcoming disappointments and hindrances, keeping always burning the interest in missions, which to them was of such infinite importance." The work of missionaries was carefully followed and jars of fruit, clothing, as well as money were sent to Home, Foreign, Freedman and Syrian Missions and to the Aged People's and Orphan's Home. Various improvements in Union's building and furnishings were also provided by these faithful women.

Thank Offering Service, still conducted by the Women's Organization today, was first held in 1889 and over the years thousands of dollars have been received for the Lord's work worldwide.

In 1908, a Young Women's Missionary Society was organized by its parent and although it disbanded in 1920, one of its members, Mrs. Alice Phillips Acheson later became a missionary to Egypt, and because of her inspiration, the Alice Acheson Circle was formed in 1933. Later it was to become a Young Women's Society.

In 1913, the women from the neighboring churches were invited to a Union meeting with the possibility of starting a Women's Christian Temperance Union (W.C.T.U.) in our community. As a result of this meeting, the Gayly W.C.T.U. was organized. It later disbanded, the members joining other similar organizations.

A number of members had the honor and privilege of attending the annual convention of the Women's General Missionary Society (W.G.M.S.) held in different parts of the United States.

Many faithful members have held office in the Women's Missionary Society but the one who excels in point of time at least, is Mrs. Ida Aiken who was elected treasurer in February 1905, having completed almost forty years of service.

THE WOMEN'S ASSOCIATION
PRESBYTERIAN WOMEN IN THE CONGREGATION

The initial planning for the Women's Association is recorded in the Session Minutes of October 11, 1958. One representative of all existing women's groups, (Loyal Daughters, Willing Workers, For Others and Kindness to All, Sunday School Classes) formed the Committee with Mrs. Leona Scott appointed as acting chairman. In January, 1959 all the women of Union were invited to join one of three Circles named in honor of Union's missionaries:

Alice Acheson—served in Egypt with husband for 40 years.

Lois Phillips—served in Philippines with husband for 8 years.

Marion Deemer—served in the Sudan with husband for 15 years.

With exception of July and August, Circles met monthly for Bible and Mission Study and quarterly together with all Circles for a special Association Meeting and were connected to Presbyterian Women at the Presbytery, Synod and Churchwide levels through meetings, workshops and conferences. One special event was the Love Feast with our sisters from Cape Fear Presbyterial in North Carolina in 1981. For many years the late Elder Ethelyn Noble was a great encouragement to the women in the Association because of her first-hand experience of missionary service in Pakistan.

Time and women's varying schedules have changed the face of the Association. We have at present one Circle with approximately twenty faithful members meeting for Prayer and Bible Study with Jackie Pfaub serving as leader. However, we have many more women who serve diligently in various activities and all under the leadership of Moderator Doris Scott, Vice Moderator, Rachel Phillips and long-time Treasurer, Virginia Wagner. A newly organized Evening Circle led by Donnelle

Glatz shows great promise for meeting the needs of working women.

Following the union of the Presbyterian Church, U.S.A. and the southern Presbyterian Church, U.S., the name of Women's Association has been changed to Presbyterian Women (PW) in the Congregation and we continue our connectionalism at Presbytery, Synod, and Churchwide levels.

Among our most important ministries are the Prayer Chain headed by Ruth Christopher, Thank Offering Service, Local Service led by Carole Campbell which encompasses bereavement dinners and various receptions, mission sewing headed by Pat Ventura, preparing food for a Soup Kitchen and Northside Seniors and supporting Meals on Wheels, World Day of Prayer and Fellowship of the Least Coin.

Union's Presbyterian Women, carrying on in the same tradition of those early Women's Missionary Society members endeavor to live up to the Presbyterian Women's Purpose:

Forgiven and Freed by God in Jesus Christ we commit ourselves:
    To nurture our faith through prayer and Bible study,
    To support the mission of the Church worldwide,
    To work for justice and peace,
    And to build an inclusive, caring, community of women that
        strengthens the Presbyterian Church (USA)
    And witness the promise of God' kingdom.

ALICE ACHESON CIRCLE

The Alice Acheson Circle for teenage girls who have outgrown the Junior society, was organized in December 1933. The Circle was named for our missionary to Egypt, Alice Phillips Acheson, who had always been a help and inspiration to the girls.

The work carried on by the members of the Circle was very similar to that of the W.M.S. Contributions were made to the seven departments of work as well as to the Young Women's Special. As part of the Thank-offering each year, some child was made a Junior Life member of the W.G.M.S. Each Christmas the girls sent a box of toys or something else that could be used in a mission station to make the season a happier one.

In 1944, the Circle expected to become a Young Women's Society in the very near future. This group is no longer active.

JUNIOR MISSIONARY SOCIETY

The Junior Missionary Society was organized for boys and girls in the community and church between the ages of six and fourteen years. Its purpose was to interest these children in sending the Gospel story to the ends of the earth and to train them for their part in that work.

A copy of the Junior Missionary Magazine was given monthly to each member of the society, subscriptions being paid for by the Women's Missionary Society. Contributions were made regularly to Home, Foreign, and Freedmen's missions and the efforts of the Juniors added splendidly to the thank-offering.

In 1894, the Juniors were organized as a Junior Y.P.C.U., but after a few years were reorganized as a Junior Missionary Society, and worked under that name. During the earlier years, the Juniors met each Sabbath evening during the summer months, but in May 1920, it was decided to hold one meeting each month throughout the year on Sabbath at the time of the morning preaching service. Many of our Juniors became Junior Life Members of the W.G.M.S. The society is no longer in existence.

YOUNG PEOPLES' CHRISTIAN UNION/YOUTH GROUP

Early in the year 1890 as reports came from all parts of the United Presbyterian Church of how the young people were organizing societies for Christian work, it was proposed that a Young Peoples' Society be organized at Union. Doubting one's thought, there was not enough talent in Union Congregation to carry on successfully such a society. Others thought the plan a good one and a few were willing to do what they could. So on Wednesday evening, May 7th, 1890, our Young Peoples' Christian Union was organized, with a membership of twenty-four.

The first prayer meeting was held on Sabbath evening, June 15th, 1890, and this society had continued to meet each Sabbath evening with very few exceptions through 1944. The membership fluctuated as the youth of the community come and go; but always, a faithful few have carried on the work that is so important in the life of the church.

Many are the boys and girls of this church and surrounding

community, who learned to give testimony for their Lord and Master and say a prayer in public at these Sabbath evening meetings; and we feel that this training has helped to take the message of Christ to the far parts of the world, since World War II has sent our boys to Africa, Asia, Australia, the islands of the sea, and also the various countries of Europe.

Officers were elected and Committees appointed following a constitution prepared by the United Presbyterian Church. Portions of the Bible and the Mission Books are studied, the Temperance Question and topics of the day are discussed at the Sabbath evening meetings. Business meetings combined with a social hour are held regularly.

Many festivals, oyster suppers and entertainments, have been given and the social life of our community has been greatly benefited by this society. Very liberal contributions have been made yearly to both Home and Foreign Missions.

Delegates have been sent to Presbyterial, State and National conventions, and also to the Missionary Conferences. Interesting reports of these meetings are brought back to the society and many are benefited by this connection with the other societies of our denomination.

The organization as it was originally known, Y.P.C.U. does not currently exist at Union church. In its place today, we have a Youth Group program. This group, composed of children from grades 7 through 12, meets on Sunday evenings, typically for an hour and a half. The group basically meets to address social and church activities. The number of attendees range from 10 to 20 in any given year. They are active at special services, such as the Christmas Eve Candlelight Service and the Easter Sunrise Service. At times, they have picnics and attend retreats. Over the years, we have attempted to conduct Youth Club programs for the 4th through 6th grade children, but the programs were abandoned for lack of participation.

PRAYER MEETING

We have already said the first attempt to organize a prayer meeting in this congregation was practically a failure. The second attempt was made the same year in which the Sabbath School was organized, that of 1859. This though not a failure, was never in a very flourishing condition. Some evenings we would have a most respectable and entertaining audience; others again we would have to fall back on the original few. Thus it went on for several years, when some of those who had stood by us in times of trials and perplexities, dropped out. We thought the best thing to do then under the circumstance was to discontinue it for a while at least; this was done. It was never reorganized, though meetings were still held occasionally. It was at last merged into the O.Y.P.C.U.

Some of those new-comers, with others of a more progressive turn of mind, undertook to establish prayer meetings in the old log church. After two or three meetings had been held, some four or five of those members of the congregation who were opposed to all religious activities of the church, attended more for curiosity than any benefit they expected to get. We are told they were so disgusted and vexed at the whole proceeding, that when the meeting was dismissed they were so mad, to put it mildly, that they walked all the way home, forgetting they had horses hitched to trees outside, upon which they had ridden there.

During the early part of Rev. Briceland's pastorate, the members of the congregation were invited to meet on Wednesday evenings at the church for the study entitled, "The Church in the Country." The outcome of this study was the dividing of the congregation into six sections for cottage prayer meetings. These meetings were held usually on Wednesday evenings and the topic for discussion was the weekly Sabbath School lesson. For a time, these meetings were well attended and were both interesting and instructive, besides contributing much to the social spirit of the community.

After a time the novelty of this plan wore off and during Rev. H. C. Hildebrand's pastorate an attempt was made to hold the prayer-meetings at the church, but without much success. So cottage prayer-meetings were held previous to communion season.

Rev. McElhinney advocated dividing the congregation into two sections for cottage prayer meetings, meeting every two weeks at different times during the year, discussing topics, or references selected by the pastor. Following this plan, meetings held were both helpful and instructive and, as a rule, very well attended.

In the more recent years, we have attempted from time to time to rekindle prayer meetings. They were conducted in the church and, as in the past, were not successful.

Along this same line, using the conveniences of the modern telephone, we have a prayer chain. There are many members of the congregation involved, and as one becomes aware of a need for prayer support, the chain is activated and through the grace of God and many prayers many wonderful things have happened.

As well, we have had church and neighborhood Bible studies throughout the recent years, but they are lightly attended. We currently publish a monthly prayer bulletin which lists the current concerns of the congregation. These are for personal use.

Over the last couple years, Rev. James Martin, Union Church's Parish Associate, conducted a week day evening Bible study. From time to time, Union church has also presented a study of the Bible using the Bethel Series. The Bethel Series teacher has been Elder Bob Pfaub. The attendance at these gatherings has been light.

K. T. A. Class

The KINDNESS TO ALL (K.T.A.) Sunday School Class was organized February 28, 1947 with more than a dozen young women of the church involved. Mrs. John (Jean) McMichael was the teacher. She served faithfully until suddenly taken by death in June, 1966.

The class name was chosen and officers were elected at the April, 1947 meeting. Meetings were held in the homes monthly except when a special activity had been planned otherwise.

The first officers elected were: President—Marian Temple; Vice President—Charlotte Mauchline; Secretary—Dorothy Provost; Treasurer—Edith White.

A Social Committee consisted of Bernice English, Elna Holden, Dorothy Malarky and Elizabeth Puhlman. There also was a Correspondence Committee appointed; Elizabeth Puhlman, Elizabeth Lloyd and Charlotte Mauchline.

Today, the class numbers about 16 and their purpose is to nurture to all by growing in their spiritual life of giving "Kindness to All" through social, charity, sympathy and concern for others.

VACATION BIBLE SCHOOL

During the summer months, since 1954, Union Church has conducted a Vacation Bible School for the young children of the church and community. The purpose of the School is to further the knowledge of the Bible. Over the most recent years, the attendance has numbered around 80 children. The School led by approximately 20 teachers and helpers, includes music and typically ends in a Friday program for the parents.

FAITHFUL FOLLOWERS

The Faithful Followers class was organized in the early 1960s and had about 20 members. The first teacher of this class of young women was Mary Ruschhaupt and the last teacher was Jessie Pearce. The purpose and theme of the class was "being faithful followers". The class ceased to exist in the mid 1970's due to the split in the church, which took some members from the class.

ADAM AND EVE
ADULT BIBLE CLASS FOR MEN AND WOMEN

This class was started around 1980 by Elder Bob Pfaub. The purpose of the class is to glorify God by studying his word. The class has about 18 regular members and it still continues today.

MOTHERS STUDY GROUP

In February 1992, Laura Duffy and Cathy Scott established a Mothers Study Group. There are 20 names on the roll and 10-12 attend the classes held on the 2nd and 4th Wednesday of the month. The purpose of the class is to enable mothers of all ages to share in fellowship and group discussions involving topics relative to the family, self esteem and spiritual giftedness. At times they have had around 18 children for which they use babysitters to care for them during the class.

PRESBYTERIAN WOMEN'S GATHERING

The Women's Gathering is the national meeting of the Presbyterian Women held every three years. This triennial meeting provides opportunity for studying, meeting and sharing with Presbyterian women from throughout the country. International visitors add a special dimension to the meetings by bringing news of the witness and work of the church worldwide. In 1991 the conference was moved from the site of many years at Purdue University, West Lafayette, Indiana to Iowa State University at Ames, Iowa. Union congregation has sent representatives to this meeting over the last 25 years.

ADULT BIBLE CLASSES

For Men and Women

This Sunday School Class was organized by Jack Howard in the mid seventies. There are 24 rostered in the class, which was started and continues today so that they may grow in the word of Christ.

Singles Class

In the spring of 1993, Rev. James Martin, started a singles class for those who are single or were previously married and now single. The class was a short term study for single or single-again people. The class of 4 to 6 completed their original planned study and then disbanded in the same spring.

Marriage and Family Class

Reverend Jim Glatz started this class in January of 1993. The class size ranges from 25-30 members. The purpose of the class is to: (1) present the biblical perspective on marriage and family, (2) discuss current issues confronting christian marriages and families and (3) provide encouragement, support and fellowship for the members of the class.

SOCIAL ACTIVITIES

Probably one of the most significant changes in the chrch has centered around social activities and affairs. As modern technology developed, more leisure time became available and social activities were on the increase. Men's groups sprang up playing softball games, dart ball matches, volleyball games and bowling as part of the church social activities. In the mid 1950's, the church held regular chicken, turkey and oyster dinners, strawberry festivals, box socials and Halloween parties for the community. These activities do not continue today.

In the more recent years, 1979 to 1986, a group held the Craft Festival for the purpose of greeting the community and raising funds. The funds helped to defray the cost of paving the parking lot and were used to purchase seat cushions for the pews. The church also has a group of women who make quilts. The quilters are making a special Bicentennial quilt with handmade cross stitch panels for the occasion.

Another area of current community involvement centers around our outreach and visition to households which are new to the area or have expressed an interest in Union Church. Lead by a member of Session, along with Reverend James Martin, who furnishes guidance and leadership, a small group of church members weekly call on these new friends to welcome them and to spread the word of the gospel in a very caring manner. Through these calls, we have increased our membership.

Every two months we prepare a church news pamphlet called the Hilltop Herald. The paper is distributed to all the church members and friends, near and far, so they can read about the church news.

Today, more and more mothers, as well as the fathers, are part of the work force. In some cases, families are raised by single parents. With this came the start of Union church's Day Care Center in 1990. It cares for children, ages infant to 6, of working parents. The center opens at 6:30 A.M. and closes at 6:30 P.M. and cares for about 50 children.

Child care playground, completed 1991.

Some children even depart from the church to go to school in the morning and return to the program in the afternoon.

One hundred years ago, on October 11, 1894, Union Church celebrated its centennial. The service lasted all day with a luncheon at noon. The first Congregational History, compiled and written by Samuel S. Glass, was read that day along with histories of the Women's Missionary Society, the Young People's Christian Union, and the Mission Band. On the occasion of the sesquicentennial in 1944, festivities began with a Community Night on October 12th, Family Night on October 13th and concluded with worship service on October 15th, 1944. Rev. Frank Davidson was the minister.

As we commemorate our bicentennial in 1994, a number of events will take place throughout the year. A surprise appearance before the congregation of "Isaac Walker," along with his Bible and rifle, petitioning for a supply of preaching will kick-off events in October 1993. A special quilt consisting of counted-cross patches representing meaningful symbols indigenous to Union Church, will be dedicated and suspended in a special area of the Church. The Quilters and other ladies in the Church have carefully and thoughtfully designed this original quilt and lovingly stitched it together.

The choir is organizing a community hymn sing. Ron Parrish, chairman of photography, put together a slide presentation to be narrated by Jacqueline and Robert Pfaub. Ron also arranged for a congregational photograph which was taken before the Church service on June 6, 1993. There were approximately 341 members present when Photographer, Jim Zaccone, snapped the picture which is duplicated in this book. Special activities for the children and youth will be held in the parking lot in June 1994. Sam Hopper has unusual surprises in store for this festive event. In May, the Upper Ohio Valley Presbyterian Historical Society will hold its annual meeting at Union. That same month a dedication of eighteen replacement tombstones of Revolutionary War veterans will be held in the cemetery. The afternoon of June 27th, bagpipers will pipe in the congregation, their friends and the community for a special service. This will be followed by an informal tea and reception. All area churches are invited to join us in the special bicentennial celebration commemorating our colorful and distinguished history.

5
Music Program

How proud and how inspired we are as we listen to our beautiful Church music. The choir, the organ music and our voices singing praises to the Lord enhance the worship service. Surprisingly, it was not always that way. Of all the changes in the worship service over the years, music has been altered the most. Two hundred years ago music was not one of the priorities in the church. There were no musical instruments allowed. In 1891, the Session relented and allowed the young people to procure an organ for their services. Finally, in 1894, the congregation was granted permission to use the organ in Sabbath morning worship.

When the present church building was completed in 1900, Andrew Carnegie donated a pipe organ. Miss Laura Bell, a member of the congregation, became the organist and remained in that position for 28 years.

The pipe organ during the 1950s became a financial burden. Many things appeared to go awry. During the early 1960s electronic organs were introduced. The first Allen organ was purchased in 1963. It was replaced in 1989 with a second Allen organ. A carillon which is programmed to ring out appropriate hymns and patriotic music to the surrounding community was added in 1988 in loving memory of Ethelyn Noble, wife of pastor Dr. Robert Noble.

The Session, at a meeting in April 1886, "elected" the following members to the "Quire": James Riddle, John Scott, Frank McCurdy and Florence McCurdy. Although choir members changed from time to time, they continued to be appointed by the Session. A Junior Choir was organized in 1897, to conduct singing in the Sabbath School. Periodically, we have enjoyed the voices of a youth choir. Today, a mixed choir of approximately 18 adults sings with dedication and enthusiasm under the direction of Carole Campbell with Cheryl Lang at the organ.

Music in our pioneer church was limited to singing of sacred songs contained in the Book of Psalms. Tune was of little importance or incidental. Some church historians have described it as "frankly deplorable —off key, off beat, and awful". There were no books or "Psalters" in 1794 in Union Church. Many members could not read and books were a rare commodity on the frontier. The singing was led by precentors who would read a line, after which the congregation would sing it and so on to the end of the Psalm. This was called "lining out the Psalms". In February, 1839, the practice of "lining" was brought before the congregation. The proposal was to try "the mode of singing without lining" for four months. Finally, in September 1849, it was resolved that "singing continuously" be established.

The General Assembly of the U.P. Church was adamant in its position on limiting singing to Psalms. The early Psalter, their song book, consisted merely of words—no music. In 1872, Union Church voted 119 to 50 in favor of using the new revised edition of the Psalter. This was the first United Presbyterian Psalter printed with music. Union Church was progressive for they were quick to purchase the new book. Notice that they were not called "Hymnals".

Apparently, not all members were satisfied. Session minutes in 1874 record that "trouble which existed between William Aikin and Alexander Spears, Samuel Scott and Jonathan Aiken, members of Session, in regard to the introduction of the new Psalms into the Church was amicably settled".

By this time, Methodists had been singing hymns and it was contagious. Our young people loved the zestful, melodic music. In fact, in October 1862, the Session "inquired of John Nicol and John McCormick concerning a 'rumor' that they had been singing hymns at Sabbath School". Mr. Nichol acknowledged that "it was wrong to sing hymns and he avoided it as much as possible". McCormick said, "What's harm in it?" And, he referred to "Book of Discipline" as a guide. These two men were ahead of their time, for it wasn't long until "Bible Songs" was published by the U.P. Church for young people. It wasn't until 1925 that the use of hymns during worship was authorized. Books of praise authorized by General Assembly have always been used in our services up until the present ones.

It has been written that the disputes over music were the most bitter ones the U.P. Church ever had. Today we smile and label this frivolous. We enjoy the toe-tapping renditions of "When the Saints Go Marching In," and other choir offerings. Wouldn't our ancestors be stunned!

6
Schism

Since time began there have been splits, differences of opinion, and dissensions at one time or another in just about every group numbering two or more. Even Cain and Abel couldn't get along; their relationship ended with very dreadful consequences. We know pretty much what happened but how do you suppose we would have acted in Cain's place? Sometimes we get stuck on the horns of our dilemma and refuse to let go, no matter what.

Churches, being composed of people, act no differently than those first people. Today, we do have all kinds of spiritual guidance from the Bible, counsel from our ministers and elders, all kinds of constitutions and bylaws, all kinds of laws and the principle of precedence(s), things that Cain didn't have, but even all those do not always bring about a peaceable meeting of the minds.

This is not to say that all disagreements or differences of opinion are bad. Not so. For without any of these most likely we would still be living in caves, hunting and gathering our food, carrying water in skins or something—well, get the picture? Change has brought us mercifully and kindly to nearly the twenty-first century. However, it is still a moot question whether we can solve all our differences of opinion in the next 2000 years. But try we certainly must!

Differences of opinion led to some very trying times at Union about twenty years ago. A Session letter, dated 4 April 1974 was sent to the Union Congregation restating publicly Rev. Broadwick's and Mr. Johovich's positions against women elders. It asked for comments from the session and the congregation. One session member replied as follows:

I believe that the Church today must live creatively in the present. And I thought maybe Union was—until recently. A few months ago when the pastor publicly stated his objection to women elders I believed Union Church was taking a giant step backwards.

It took some twenty or more centuries to free all the slaves. And Paul, not once but several times (i.e. Eph. 6: 5ff) counseled the slaves to submit willingly to the yoke as to the King. No doubt this was necessary or expedient at that time, in that society, but please not in the twentieth century. (Added at this writing: We Christians are still to submit to the yoke of Christ the King, but there are technical and theological differences between the two types of slaves.)

It took 72 years for women to get the political right to vote in the United States, from 1848 to 1920. Yet I hardly think anyone in his right mind today would try to get this repealed. . . . in addition I oppose calling Randy Johovich as Assistant Minister because he now also espouses this same archaic viewpoint. I do not believe in perpetuating such a ministry at Union. . . .

This preamble led to a big difference of opinion at Union Church, starting sometime prior to 1974. As early as 1972, there were mumblings of objections to women serving as elders; the first by the session moderator, followed soon by many members of the then current session. Union Church had earlier been associated with Presbyterian bodies which did not approve of women elders or ministers. Because of that, Mr. Broadwick and the session certainly had precedence on their side.

This viewpoint now was contrary to the Book of Order of the Presbyterian Church in the USA which had granted women the right to serve as elders as far back as 1930, and to serve as teaching elders or ministers, in 1956. A decision of the Permanent Judicial Commission of the General Assembly in support of women elders, said:

Our understanding of the Church's mission has grown with time, . . . our Church, a living and changing institution, has so defined its mission that a candidate (for ministry) who says it is in error in ordaining women, compromises his affirmative answers to these questions in his ordination vows:

No. 3. Will you be instructed by the confessions of our Church and led by them as you lead the people of God?

No. 4. Will you be a minister of the Word in obedience to Jesus Christ, under the authority of Scripture, and continually be guided by our confessions?

No. 6. Will you govern the way you live, by following the Lord Jesus Christ, loving neighbors, and working for the reconciliation of the world?

Mr. Broadwick had *already given his affirmative answers* to these questions in his ordination 16 July, 1967, and Mr. Johovich had to look forward to assenting to them before he could be ordained!

Both of them gave as their principal reason for their great concern for Union Church's spiritual well-being the fact that the Book of Order now mandated that women be permitted to serve as elders or ministers. This, they strongly argued, was against Scriptures, especially I Timothy 2:11-14 and I Corinthians 14:34.

Now, about these scriptural passages much has been written, and argued, both pro and con. The consensus of a great number of scholars is that I Corinthians 14:34 seems to be a later insertion and not of Pauline origin, since it appears at different places in different Greek manuscripts of the New Testament. It is believed it pertains to the behavior of wives and *not women generally*, as the Greek shows. What it specifically forbids is their interruption of the worship service by asking questions in the midst of preaching. Similarly, the I Timothy passage; it is also thought, was directed at a particular problem in the Ephesian Church. Elsewhere, in the same letter, Paul takes it for granted that women will pray and prophesy (a form of preaching!) in the worship service (I Cor. 11:5). The above clarification is condensed from the report of an ad hoc sub-committee dated May 13, 1974, a copy of which must have assuredly been sent to Mr. Broadwick. Nevertheless, Messrs. Broadwick and Johovich continued to maintain their position, despite a letter from Pittsburgh Presbytery which stated:

> It is our opinion that Mr. Broadwick should actively concur with the Church's opinion on ordaining women. If he cannot do this, he should passively submit and cease trying to influence the congregation in this matter. If he cannot do this, he should peaceably withdraw from our communion without trying to make any schism.
> Signed Sub-Committee members,
> Geo. S. Wilson, Rec. Sec'y.

Subsequently, this information was sent to Union Church members in a letter of 8 January 1975 from Mr. Broadwick, stating, "I have made the very painful decision to seek release from the United Presbyterian Church in the United Sates of America's Denomination in the near future to become a part of a Denomination wherein my views are honored and acceptable... neither Randy nor myself have precipitated the problems.... Further, Randy and I are anxious to communicate the fact that we dearly love the people and ministry of Union Church...."

This letter was followed 15 January 1975, with another from the session stating, "Your Session has responded to this crisis situation...by deciding to recommend to the Congregation... that Union petition Pittsburgh Presbytery to release her and *her real property* to the care and ministry of the Mid-Atlantic Presbytery of the Presbyterian Church in America....

Attached to this 15 January letter was a two and a quarter page Resolution with thirteen "whereas's" outlining the points stated above and other complaints, ending with a "Therefore", "that the Congregation respectfully and lovingly in Christ Jesus our Lord, request the Presbytery of Pittsburgh to transfer us *with our real property (which we are willing to purchase from the United Presbyterian Church in the USA at a negotiated* sum agreeable to both parties) to the care and ministry of the Mid-Atlantic Presbytery of the Presbyterian Church in America, such transfer to take final effect upon our formal receipt as a congregation into membership of that Presbytery and Denomination." So the gauntlet was thrown down!

Union Presbyterian Church

Mr. Broadwick and the majority part of the session were told by the minority part at nearly every session meeting, from 1972 'til 1975, they didn't need to petition for release from Pittsburgh Presbytery — all they needed to do was walk away. But they insisted this Resolution be presented at an Ecclesiastical/Congregational meeting on 23 January, 1975. If it were passed by the Congregation it would then be presented to Pittsburgh Presbytery for its consideration.

At the meeting, the Resolution was read to the Congregation and a motion was made and seconded that it be adopted. In the discussion that followed, two elders spoke for the motion and two against. The last elder speaking said:

> I want to speak against the motion and point out some of the consequences if you pass it.
>
> First, if you pass it you will be a Congregation without a home here. One very good authority says there is no way, no way, you can get the property. You can remonstrate, cry, even sue, but you can't get the property.
>
> Secondly, the PCA is a schismatic group which thrives on division as it has divided us. Latest reports say it is almost bankrupt.
>
> Thirdly, and much more importantly, the motion as presented has a far greater implication on your faith. It is in part anti-Biblical and contrary to two of the primary Christian laws we profess to believe in. I'm referring to two of the Ten Commandments, numbers ten and eight. The motion is in direct violation of number ten which states: Thou shall not covet. Certainly those in favor of the motion want the Church property so badly they, seemingly, are willing to sell their souls for it.
>
> Fourthly, if passed, it will be a violation of the eighth commandment which states: Thou shalt not steal. For the clandestine and secretive manner that causes us to meet on this sorry night for this purpose, I say, is stealing.

So don't talk to me with words of love on your lips when there is larceny in your hearts. A vote against the motion will keep your souls pure. God loves you and wants you for his own. Turn your back on sin.

There was a slight burst of applause as he sat down. One of the commission members was heard to say, "Well, there you have both the legality and morality of the situation."

At that point, Leona Scott questioned whether the motion wasn't illegal and unconstitutional. The Moderator, Rev. Douglas Dunderdale, ruled that the motion was unconstitutional per the Stated Clerk, William Thompson. However, Mr. Thompson said that a majority of the congregation could overturn this ruling and allow consideration of the motion to take place. The vote was 192 to overturn the ruling and 130 against overturning. A secret ballot on the main motion was taken, overseen by a member of each side, with the counting being handled by the Administrative Commission. The vote for withdrawing was 128, against 209. So the schism was accomplished! But not to everyone's satisfaction. Both sides lost! During the counting of the ballots the question of removal of members and inactive member notices was raised. The clerk defended the severe pruning of the rolls as being long overdue. These were the figures:

	1970	1971	1972	1973	1974
Members, Jan.	695	589	582	587	564
Add by Profession of Faith, Reaffirmation	16	19	27	18	18
Add by Certificate	18	17	18	20	9
Lost by Certificate	25	17	9	16	15
Other Session Removal	112	19	18	39	15
Transfer to Inactive					*24
Deaths		3	7	7	6
Total, December	589	582	587	564	534
Difference (Loss)	(106)	(7)	5	(23)	(30)

*The Session had voted to transfer to the inactive list the 24 above marked with an asterisk on December 17, 1974. Many of those on the list complained they were not notified until a few days before the vote.

Union Presbyterian Church 65

The compass course on which the Session majority was embarked can be somewhat deduced from the annual reports of 1974 given to the session, by: The Student Assistant: among other things he reported attendance at Reformed Fellowship Meetings; attendance at National Presbyterian Reformed Fellowship 10/24/74. The pastor's Report; Among other things, Meetings of Reformed Fellowship, 13; luncheon meeting of National Presbyterian and Reformed Fellowship 2/24/74; Holy Land Trip/Study leave; preached at Butler and Philadelphia 8/1 and 8/18/74; study leave to go to the General Assembly Meeting of the Presbyterian Church in America at Macon, Georgia, 9/18 to 9/20/74; organized and participated in the "Popular Meeting" of the National Presbyterian and Reformed Fellowship at Union Church, 10/24/74.

A bright ray of hope came out of all this, proving that God's in His Heaven and still showering us with His blessings. Within a few weeks after the "vote" Union had regrouped, reorganized and redeployed its people to fill the ranks and carry on the Lord's work on our hill. With renewed spirit and dedication a new choir was organized. Volunteers stepped forward to reorganize and teach Sunday School. New Elders, Deacons and Trustees were quickly elected from the nucleus of 421 members remaining with Union Church. We were marching forward in the faith of our forefathers. They had faced adversity before and with God's help came shining through. This is the true spirit of Union Church. God Bless Us All!

This writer hopes we never have to go through this again! Just, perhaps, Galations 3:28-29 can help prevent that: "There is neither Jew nor Greek, slave nor free, male nor female, for you are all one in Christ Jesus. If you belong to Christ, then you are Abraham's seed and heirs according to the promise." So be it!

7
Denominational Mergers

Union Church takes great pride in our denomination, Presbyterian Church (U.S.A.), and the influence it has generated in our country and throughout the world. There have been many mergers with other Presbyterian denominations in our 200 year history. In 1782, the Associate Presbyterians (Seceders) and Reformed Presbyterians (Covenanters) adopted a basis of union and the new Associate Reformed Church of North America was organized. Twelve years later, in 1794, Union Church became part of that body. The concrete tablet in Fellowship Hall with initials A.R. attests to our affiliation. This denomination spread rapidly, especially in Pennsylvania and in the Pittsburgh area.

Over the years some of the Associate Presbyterian churches who had rejected the initial jointure in 1782, began negotiations with the A.R. Church. Agreements between the two denominations were reached in 1858 and the Church union was consummated in a historic ceremony in Pittsburgh, PA. The banner unfurled reading "The Truth of God" on one side and the other proclaimed "Forbearance in Love". These beautiful words were the motto of the newly formed United Presbyterian Church of North America for 100 years. Union Church was part of that flourishing denomination.

Presbyterians historically have strived for unity. It took another hundred years before the United Presbyterian Church of North America and the Presbyterian Church in the U.S.A. united in 1958, to form the United Presbyterian Church in the U.S.A. What a stir this caused in Union Church! One apprehension of the old U.P.'s was that they would be swallowed-up by the much larger denomination. They were comfortable with their friendly little denomination spread around the country. There was a unique bonding with familiar names and faces of our ministers and of our missionaries.

As plans for merger proceeded, each Presbytery was asked to vote on the "Plan for Union". In 1956, the old Monongahela Presbytery met at Union Church to argue the merits and to vote on that issue. Our sanctuary was filled with dignified Elders and Ministers with our former pastor, Rev. William Ruschhaupt, as Moderator. One distinguished gentleman rose and declaimed, "I'm U.P. born and U.P. bred. When I die there will be a U.P. dead". There were no doubts about his vote!

Despite misgivings of many devout U.P.'s, merger was inevitable. Again, the historic ceremony took place in Pittsburgh, with formal ceremonies culminating the event at the old Syria Mosque in Oakland. We were now part of a much larger denomination.

Keeping the spirit of unity alive, another 25 years passed when we merged again. For many years the United Presbyterian Church (Northern) hoped to forge a reunion with the Presbyterian Church in the United States (Southern). That church had withdrawn from several organized Presbyterian groups around 1861, when anti-slavery resolutions were passed. Finally, on June 10, 1983, in Atlanta, Georgia, our United Presbyterian Church in the United States of America and the Presbyterian Church (U.S.) merged to become the Presbyterian Church (U.S.A.) ending 120 years of separation.

Perhaps Union's most unusual merger took place around 1816, before the existence of our oligraphic records. From the Minutes of the Correspondent of the Reformed Dissenting Presbyterian Congregations, edited by Dr. Reid Stewart, we learn that a small group of Associate Reformed Presbyterians disagreed with their Synod action altering and modifying the Confession of Faith. Consequently, in 1801, they organized the Reformed Dissenting Presbytery. Minutes of the Correspondent indicate two of these congregations were within the boundaries of Robinson Township—one on Campbell's Run Road and the other at Moon Run. Names of their members appear in these minutes, and some of the same names later turn up on Union Church rolls.

Our early church histories describe a communion held in 1805 on the farm of Samuel Scott, when 50 or 60 people attended. Mr. Scott's farm was located on Campbell's Run Road. Accounts of this communion can be found in the Scott family history and in several other sources including Dr. Thomas Spoull's article in The Reformed Presbyterian and

Covenantor published in October, 1875. It is certain that a communion was held on the Scott farm in 1805, but it was not a Union Church service. The ministers officiating have been identified as a "Rev. Gilmore" and Dr. S. B. Wylie. Both ministers were ineligible to hold communion services in the Associate Reformed Church, namely, Union Church. In addition, Union had its own minister, Dr. John Riddell, and we also had our own church building. There would have been no reason to hold a communion elsewhere.

The Reformed Dissenting Presbyterian group did not exist for any length of time. They endeavored to affiliate with the Reformed Presbyterian Church as early as 1806 but were denied. They finally merged with the Associate Synod of North America in 1851. Local members probably affiliated with Union about 1816 (when we officially adopted that name). The Samuel Scott family later played a prominent role in Union's history and his ancestors can be found on our Church rolls today. Can you think of a better name than "Union" for two adjacent congregations of similar creeds and heritage when they become one church?

Considering the changes in our society, the economic upheaval, the new vitality of non-Christian faiths in the past decade, the Church has a tremendous mission ahead. We have attempted to resolve and deal with painful problems. The Church has not closed its eyes to the evils of society. Although we raise our eyebrows and gasp at some decisions, we must also be grateful that the leaders of our denomination are coming to grips with major crises. It is certain there will be future mergers. Our reactions will be the same, apprehension and anxiety. Ultimately, we will submerge our desires to that which is best for Christian brotherhood and unity.

As the Church moves forward, we should be guided by the prayer that constituted the 1983 Atlanta Assembly, "Almighty God . . . be with members of our General Assembly. Help them to welcome new things you are doing in the world, and to respect old things you keep and use. Save them from empty slogans or senseless controversy."

8
Pastors

REV. JOHN RIDDELL

The first pastor of this organization, was born in County Monaghan, Ireland, in 1757, was graduated at Glasgow University, Scotland, in 1792, and studied theology in the Burgher Hall, under the care of John Brown, of Haddington; was licensed June 14th, 1788, and ordained on the 18th day of November, in the same year, by the Presbytery of Monaghan (Burgher); was pastor of the congregation of Donaghcloney, in County Down, November, 1788-93. He resigned this charge and immediately emigrated to the United States, and on the 14th of May, 1794, was received by the Associate Reformed Presbytery of Monongahela, and accepted, the same day, a call from the united congregations of Robinson Run and Steep Hollow, and was installed pastor of same August 15th, 1794. He resigned Lower Branch September 11th, 1816, retaining the other, Robinson Run, until his death, which occurred September 4th, 1829, in his 71st year. Mr. Riddell was quite a small man, with piercing black eyes. He was a man of great energy and perseverance. He was clerk of Monongahela Presbytery until shortly before his death. Presbytery meetings took him away from home for days at a time as he traveled great distances on horseback to reach designated churches. Mr. Riddell served as trustee of Canonsburg Academy from 1798-1802. The following year he held the same position with Jefferson College resigning in 1805. Though fearless and independent in his ways of thinking, he always had the good will and respect of those with whom he came in contact. Dr. Riddell was ahead of his time in his broad interpretation of the scripture. Apparently his opinion and interpretations of the Bible were widely respected by his contemporaries. In an "informal private discussion" with Alexander Campbell, founder of the Disciples of

Christ and later the Christian Church, Mr. Riddell admitted that there is no direct authority in the scripture for infant baptism. He was brave in offering this interpretation, for infant baptism was a doctrine of the Associate Reformed Church. He was not only very much attached to the distinctive principles of his denomination, but also to his congregation and the surrounding community. His home was near Gregg's crossing. Many a time he, on foot or horseback, traveled over these hills and valleys, preaching the gospel, visiting the sick, comforting the lonely and distressed, and when need required, helping bury their dead. His labors were not without reward. He was buried in Robinson Run Cemetery. His body was hauled to the grave on the fore-carriage of a common road wagon. Dr. Riddle was pastor of this congregation 22 years and 21 days.

REV. MOSES KERR

The second pastor of this organization, or rather we might say the first pastor of Union congregation, was born in Ballygoney in the county of Tyrone, Ireland, in the year 1770, where his father, Joseph Kerr, preached. He was ordained and installed pastor of a congregation in County Antrim, in Burgher Presbytery, in 1790. He resigned this charge in 1818 and emigrated to America, and in the same year connected himself with the Associate Reformed Presbytery of Monongahela, and soon after, March 17th, 1819, received a call from Union; was installed pastor May 5th of the same year; resigned the pastorate of Union November, 1827; went to Rocky Spring and New Brighton, PA, September 5th, 1828, and there remained until his death, October 11th, 1830, in his 60th year. Mr. Kerr was a man above the ordinary size, both mentally and physically. He was a very successful pastor, had many warm friends in Union congregation and the community at large. Rev. Moses Kerr was pastor of Union congregation 8 years, 3 months and 27 days.

REV. ANDREW S. FULTON

The third pastor of Union congregation, was born in Allegheny County, PA, in 1805; was graduated at the Western University in 1828, and studied theology at Allegheny; was licensed April 27th, 1831, by Monongahela Presbytery; was ordained and installed pastor of Union, May 28th, 1833, by the same; resigned the pastorate of

Union congregation August 17th, 1839. He went to Peoria, IL, 1839-43. He died at Tarentum, PA, March 10th, 1845, in his 40th year. Mr. Fulton was a man of very small stature, quick, high tempered, and of a very excitable nature; a good preacher, better preacher than pastor accordingly. Rev. Andrew S. Fulton was pastor of Union congregation 5 years, 8 months and 11 days.

REV. JOHN EKIN, D.D.

The fourth pastor of Union congregation was born February 15th, 1812, in Westmoreland County, PA; was graduated at the Western University in 1835, and studied theology at Allegheny; was licensed April 11th, 1838, by Monongahela Presbytery, and ordained by the same May 2d, 1839. He was pastor of the Second Associate Reformed Church, Pittsburgh, from May until August, 1839. He was installed pastor of Union December 11th, 1839; resigned the pastorate of Union congregation December 22d, 1853. He went to the First Associate Reformed Church, Pittsburgh, 1854-57; LeClair, Iowa, 1857-59; Monroe, in Louisiana, 1859-63; Topeka, Kansas, 1869, where he died, September 30th, 1869, in his 57th year. Dr. Ekin was a man above the ordinary stature, straight, prepossessing, of commanding manners and pleasing eloquence, a most successful and beloved pastor. Rev. John Ekin, D.D., was pastor of Union congregation 14 years and 11 days.

REV. WILLIAM MCMILLIN

The fifth pastor of Union congregation, was born in Pittsburgh, Allegheny County, PA, April 6th, 1826; graduated at Duquesne College, Pittsburgh, in 1847, and studied theology at Allegheny; was licensed March 27th, 1850, by Monongahela Presbytery, and ordained November 2d, 1853, by Boston Presbytery. He was pastor at Lowell, MA, 1853-54; was installed pastor of Union, February 5th, 1855; resigned the pastorate of Union congregation June 16th, 1857. He went to Hamilton, OH, 1858-64; Circleville, OH, 1864-80. Mr. McMillin was a small man, compactly built, with a pleasing countenance of small extreme features; he used the most florid eloquence of speech, was an able preacher, but owing to his difficulty of hearing was not a very successful pastor. Rev. Wm. McMillin was pastor of Union congregation 2 years, 4 months and 11 days.

REV. LAFAYETTE MARKS, D.D.

The sixth pastor of Union congregation, was born in Robinson Township, Allegheny County, PA, in 1838; graduated at Franklin College in 1856, and studied theology at Allegheny; was licensed by Monongahela Presbytery, April 13th, 1859; was ordained and installed pastor of Union, by the same, April 10th, 1860; resigned the pastorate of Union congregation, March 26th, 1867. He went to Wilmington, Delaware, 1867.

Mr. Marks was one of the most polished orators Union congregation ever had as a pastor. Rev. Lafayette Marks was pastor of Union congregation 6 years, 11 months and 16 days.

REV. JAMES D. TURNER

The seventh pastor of Union congregation, was born February 26th, 1834, at Wilkinsburg, Allegheny County, PA; was graduated at Franklin College in 1857, and studied theology at Allegheny; was licensed by Monongahela Presbytery, September 26th, 1860; ordained and installed pastor in Cincinnati, OH, by First Ohio Presbytery, October 10th, 1861-67; resigned this charge, March, 1868; installed pastor of Union congregation February 13th, 1868; resigned the pastorate of Union congregation, June 30th, 1874. He went to East Eleventh Street, NY, August 26th, 1874-78; Fourth Church, Pittsburgh, 1878. Mr. Turner was one of the most successful, beloved and worthy pastors Union congregation ever had.

Rev. James D. Turner was pastor of Union congregation, 6 years, 3 months and 25 days.

REV. JOHN A. DOUTHETT

The eighth pastor of Union congregation, was born in Butler County, PA, May 19, 1851; was graduated at Westminster in 1873, and studied theology at Allegheny; was licensed February 9th, 1876, by Frankford Presbytery; was ordained and installed pastor of Union, by Monongahela Presbytery, November 14th, 1876, resigned the pastorate of Union congregation June 26th, 1894. He went to Greensburg, Westmoreland County, PA. It was said that Mr. Douthett was one of the best, most original and outspoken pastors ever settled over Union congregation or in this community.

Rev. John A. Douthett was pastor of Union congregation 17 years, 7 months and 12 days.

REV. JOHN T. AIKIN

Rev. John T. Aikin, the ninth pastor of Union congregation was born in Tuscarawas County, OH, March 21, 1869. In 1894, he was graduated from Muskingum College and from the Theological Seminary at Pittsburgh in 1897. He was licensed to preach by Muskingum Presbytery, April 7, 1896. He was called by Union Congregation to be their pastor, and was ordained and installed in this church, June 29, 1897. He resigned as pastor of this congregation, June 28, 1904. His other pastorates were as follows: Rochester, PA, July, 1904 to July, 1912; Wilmerding, PA, July, 1912 to February, 1916; Rushville, IN, February, 1916 to January, 1921; Aurora, IL, stated supply, January, 1921 to April, 1922; Hebron, IN, April 1922 to November 1924; Columbia City, IA, November, 1924-1929; Deer Creek, PA, December 17, 1929 to 1932, and died that year. He preached the Word in its purity and simplicity, and was a faithful pastor. In the homes where there was sickness or bereavement, he was a true friend. He was pastor of Union congregation seven years.

REV. JAMES M. BRICELAND

Rev. James M. Briceland, the tenth pastor of Union Congregation was born at Hickory, Washington County, PA, June 29, 1876. He graduated from Westminster College in 1902. He entered the Pittsburgh Theological Seminary and was graduated in 1905, and was licensed to preach by Monongahela Presbytery in the same year. On June 27, 1905, he was ordained and installed pastor of Union congregation. He was released from this pastorate, September 1, 1914, and became pastor of the First United Presbyterian Church, Butler, PA, in 1914, remaining there until 1917. He was pastor of Parkers' Landing Presbyterian Church from 1917-1924 and Sheraden Presbyterian Church from 1924-1929. On June 1, 1929, he became pastor of the Federated Church at Sheraden. Rev. Briceland died in 1943. He was pastor of Union congregation 9 years.

REV. H. C. HILDEBRAND

Rev. H. C. Hildebrand, the eleventh pastor of Union congregation, was born at Greenville, PA, October 23, 1877. He was graduated from Westminster College in 1903 and from Pittsburgh Theological Seminary in 1906. He was licensed to preach at Jamestown, PA, December 12, 1905, by Lake Presbytery. He was ordained by Lake Presbytery and installed pastor at Linesville, PA, June 6, 1906, and was released November 4, 1908. He was pastor of Harmony United Presbyterian Church from December 8, 1908, to October 12, 1915. He was installed pastor of Union Congregation on January 18, 1916 and released August 31, 1925, to go to the First Church of Canton, Ohio. Here he was installed October 6, 1925 and resigned in 1941. He died August 13, 1946. He was pastor of Union's congregation for 9 years.

REV. J. HOY McELHINNEY

Rev. J. Hoy McElhinney, the twelfth pastor of Union congregation was born in Minden, Nebraska, March 14, 1893. He graduated from Monmouth College, in June, 1916. In the fall of 1916, he entered the Pittsburgh Theological Seminary, graduating in 1919. He was licensed to preach by Keokuk Presbytery. He was ordained, July 8, 1919 and installed pastor of Burlington, Iowa, United Presbyterian Church, where he remained until December 23, 1923. He held the pastorate at North Bend, Nebraska, from January 18, 1924 to June 6, 1926. July 9, 1926, he became pastor of Union United Presbyterian Church. It was during this pastorate that Moon Run Presbyterian Church reorganized as Moon Run United Presbyterian Church. He was released in 1937 and was pastor of Union 11 years.

REV. FRANK DAVIDSON

Rev. Frank Davidson, the thirteenth pastor of Union Congregation was born August 6, 1883, in Callery, PA, Butler County. He attended Westminster College, where he received his degree. He attended Pittsburgh-Xenia Seminary. He served as pastor at the United Presbyterian Church of Johnstown, New York. Before his call to Union, he was pastor of the United Presbyterian Church of Walton, New York for seventeen years. He received his call to Union congregation

September 15, 1938, and served until 1945. He died in March 1946 in the parsonage of Union Church. The Union session voted to pay $483 for Rev. Davidson's burial at Union Cemetery. He lived his life as a devout Christian and had much patience. He was a forceful pastor of righteousness and he followed the Holy Spirit. He was pastor of Union congregation 8 years.

REV. DR. WILLIAM F. RUSCHHAUPT, JR.

Rev. William F. Ruschhaupt, the fourteenth pastor of Union congregation, was born at Allen, PA, October 2, 1908. He graduated from Muskingum College in 1936. He was ordained to the ministry of the Presbyterian Church (formerly the United Presbyterian Church) in 1939 and installed as pastor of Hampton Presbyterian Church from 1939 until released in 1942. He served as U.S. Army Chaplain of the 3rd Engineering Brigade in the South Pacific from 1942 until 1946, and received the bronze star. He was called and installed pastor to Union congregation in 1946. During that period of pastorate he served 18 months in the Korean conflict and returned as pastor to Union congregation. He was released from his call in 1961. He served at Pittsburgh Presbytery as Executive Presbyter from 1962 to 1978, from which he retired. He was the first President of Council of Bishops and Executives of Christian Associates of Southwestern Pennsylvania. He was a dynamite pastor, tall in stature with a caring personality. He was pastor of Union congregation 15 years.

REV. WILLIAM C. COOK

Rev. William C. Cook, the fifteenth pastor of Union congregation was born in Shaler Township, PA, February 4, 1928. He graduated from Westminster College, B.A., 1952. He attended Pittsburgh-Xenia Seminary and graduated in 1955; ordained at Kiskiminetas United Presbyterian Church in 1955; served as pastor of Trinity United Presbyterian Church from 1955 to 1961. He was called to Union congregation November 19, 1961 and released in October 1969. During the summer of 1959 he toured the Holy Land. He encouraged vigorous programs for the young people and was a well versed pastor following the word of the Bible. After leaving Union, Rev. Cook was the Associate

Director of Educational Services for Pittsburgh Presbytery. He continued to work for the Presbyterian Church in Florida. He was later killed in a tragic automobile accident on his way to work on October 3, 1985. He was pastor of Union congregation for 8 years.

REV. ARTHUR BROADWICK

Rev. Arthur Broadwick, the sixteenth pastor of Union congregation was born at Allentown, PA, 1936. He attended Muhlenberg College in Allentown, PA and graduated June 1957 B.S.B.A. He attended Westminster Theological Seminary, Philadelphia, PA from September 1963 to May 1966, and Pittsburgh Theological Seminary from September 1966 to May 1967, when he graduated with a Master of Divinity Degree. He was ordained as minister by West Jersey Presbytery in July 1967. He served from 1967 to 1969 as pastor of Center Presbyterian Church in New Castle, PA. He was pastor of Union Congregation from May 1969 to February 1975. At that time, he forced a split in the church during which he tried to form his own church. He was released from Union congregation in 1975 and formed the Providence Presbyterian Church (PCA) of Robinson Township, PA in 1975. He was pastor of Union congregation 6 years.

REV. DR. ROBERT E. NOBLE

Rev. Robert E. Noble, the seventeenth pastor of Union congregation was born and raised in Crafton, PA. After a period of service with the U.S. Marine Corp, he attended Westminster College and received a B.A. Degree. He was selected by a Board of Foreign Missions to teach in Rawalpindi, Pakistan. He returned to the United States in 1951 and entered Pittsburgh-Xenia Seminary. He received a Th. M. degree in Theology. He was ordained pastor of First United Presbyterian Church of Apollo, PA. In 1957 he was appointed career missionary and assigned to Pakistan. In 1968, he organized a new congregation called Protestant International Congregation and became its first pastor. In 1976, he was called to Union congregation and served as pastor until October 1990 from whence he retired. He was caring and nurturing and family oriented. He enjoyed a wide circle of friends and was well liked in the community. He was pastor of Union congregation for 14 years.

REV. JAMES F. MARTIN
(Parish Associate)

Rev. James F. Martin, a graduate of Gordon-Conwell Seminary, came to us in 1989 (after serving interim pastorates at First U.P. Church of Boston and Leetsdale Presbyterian Church), to assist Rev. Noble. He has led several bible studies, Sunday School classes, helped in our outreach and visitation programs, while persuing his doctorate at Duquesne University.

REV. JACK M. BOWERS
(Interim Pastor)

Rev. Jack M. Bowers was invited from Pittsburgh Presbytery to guide us following Rev. Robert Noble's retirement. Rev. Bowers served from February 1991 until he was released in October 1992. His educational background includes degrees from Purdue University, McCormick Theological Seminary, Chicago and University of Pittsburgh. He spent 30 years as Minister of Christian Education and 13-1/2 years at Hebron Presbyterian Church as Associate pastor. He served Union congregation for 1 year and 6 months.

REV. DR. JAMES D. GLATZ

Rev. James D. Glatz is the eighteenth pastor of Union congregation. He was born October 17, 1956. He attended Geneva College and graduated from Union Theological Seminary in Virginia in 1983, Master of Divinity. He is currently enrolled in Doctor of Ministry at Union Seminary. He served Montrose Presbyterian Church, Richmond, VA from 1989—1992. He received the call to Union Congregation October 1, 1992, and is presently serving as pastor of Union congregation as this history is being prepared.

Church congregation, 1944 Sesquicentennial.

Afterword

*"For I dipt into the future, far as human eye could see,
Saw the Vision of the world, and all the wonder that
would be...."*

Tennyson

THROUGH THE YEARS

Today as we "dip" into the past and reflect on the first families of Union Church plodding over Pennsylvania's rough terrain on foot with their meager possessions, we are amazed at their strength and fortitude. It took months to make the journey across the mountains and valleys. Surely, God was with them and they knew it! Later, immigrants to this area were fortunate to come in Conestoga wagons, canal boats, steam engines and automobiles. Now we "jet" in to the magnificent new airport easily seen from our hilltop home.

The days of walking barefoot to Church, with shoes in a knapsack until Church was reached, are long gone. The horse and buggy soon brought worshippers over rutted, sometimes muddy, one lane roads. The Steubenville Pike was built in 1802 and that provided some improvement. The old sheds for housing buggies were not torn down until the early 1920's and then it was to the great consternation of some members of the Congregation. Horses were replaced by Model T Fords, only to be replaced by the sleek autos of today driving over super highways which criss-cross our local area.

Nowadays, we talk about "shopping" for groceries or other supplies. In the horse and buggy era, the word was "trade", and it literally meant that. Specie was rare in Western Pennsylvania and residents bartered for supplies. Monongahela whiskey was always good for exchange. Even ministers were paid by members furnishing staples plus chickens, eggs, butter, vegetables, whiskey and oats for horses.

Although the first mail service between Pittsburgh and Philadelphia began in 1788, it took at least a month to receive communications. Packhorses could make the trip in 20 days. How exciting it must have been in 1896 when the rural free delivery service began. Mail arrived directly at your residence! Communication improved with the telephone. The Gayly Local Telephone Company incorporated in 1903. Pearl Riddle, a life-long member of Union Congregation, was its first operator. Later, in 1964, when Bell Telephone built its new facility on the former S. H. and J. A. Scott farm, Pearl was honored for her contribution. We seldom hear of operators these days. Everything has been replaced by the computer, and the old oak wall phone is a treasured antique.

The one room school house organized and taught by Alexander Phillips in 1836, and filled with Presbyterian pupils has been supplanted by huge academic complexes. Reading, writing and arithmetic have had to make room for technology and sophisticated computer sciences. School prayer and Bible reading, once an integral part of the school day, were deemed unacceptable on the basis of separation of church and state. Presbyterians emphasized a sound education. It was important to read and write to understand the Bible. This is affirmed by the number of early "academies" in this area governed by boards comprised of Presbyterian men—many from Union Church.

Our earliest members worshiped in a rustic log church without the creature comforts we enjoy today. As we walk into our beautiful sanctuary, we are greeted with a friendly handshake, then an usher finds us a comfortable pew covered with a "Presbyterian blue" cushion. Approval for ushers was given by Session in 1898. Adequate and discreet lighting, heating and the sound system are designed to enhance our enjoyment of the Sunday service. Large print Bibles are available as are listening devices for the hearing impaired. One of our younger members, Vicky Ruth Harmasch, is the interpreter for the deaf during the service. A recorded message of the Sunday service is available to our shut-ins. Those early members would think we were really getting soft!

Not only did the comfort factor increase; so have our numbers. When Isaac Walker petitioned Monongahela Presbytery in 1793 for a

Union Presbyterian Church

minister to "Steep Hollow", we are told there were approximately 15 families and 35 members. Ten years later, Rev. Riddell reported to Presbytery that his two congregations (Robinson Run was his second charge) numbered 125 families and 260 adults. We can assume half of these numbers belonged to "Steep Hollow". By 1851, the congregation had doubled, and more than 100 years later, in 1967, under Rev. William Cook, families numbered 300 with a membership of 702. Today, we have 260 families on our church roll with about 500 members.

An educated ministry is a mark of the Presbyterian Church, so it is not surprising to learn that Pittsburgh Seminary had its roots a short distance away in Beaver County in the vicinity of Service Creek. The Seminary was established in 1794 by Rev. John Anderson, who was the sole instructor. Students came from as far away as New York and Eastern Pennsylvania to study theology and to become ministers in the Presbyterian Church. Previous to this all ministers arrived here from Scotland or Ireland. The Presbyterian Church had a dire need for pastors since congregations were being organized rapidly on the frontier.

Our National Shrine, the Cemetery, attests to the brave men of Union who fought in eight wars through the 200 years we are observing. There are 24 Revolutionary War veterans buried in Union. Eighteen replacement tombstones identifying the graves of Revolutionary War veterans were provided by the federal government in 1993. The service of 13 of these valiant men had not been listed in our previous history books. This affirms the great patriots who were in this part of Pennsylvania and their willingness to fight for independence.

Time has been a significant factor. In the early days it was not unusual to have the service last most of the day with Communion lasting three days. As members became restless, they could take a break and walk about. It wasn't long until services were shortened. In 1898, "preaching began at 10:30 instead of 11:00 a.m.", according to session minutes. Sixteen years later in 1914, they voted to hold opening exercises of Sunday School immediately after "preaching service" with no intermission. Something must have gone awry in 1916, for a committee was appointed "to look after the disorder in the Sunday School room during preaching". The Church service preceded Sabbath School until 1966, when we returned to the 11:00 a.m. service.

A genuine time problem existed before 1883, when Standard time was adopted over the entire United States. Today, it is hard for us to imagine the confusion that occurred before the system was put into effect. Each local town or village had its own "sun" time. In the Pittsburgh area there were six different time standards. Let us hope all Union members used "Gayly sun time".

Farming was the chief occupation of Union's members until after World War II, when Indian Pines and other housing plans were developed. Under the leadership of Dr. Ruschhaupt, who was pastor at this time, membership increased rapidly. Veterans returning from the war married their sweethearts and were ready to settle down. The new members represented a wide variety of occupations. Gradually, the old farms of Robinson Township gave way to housing, shopping centers, industrial parks, banks, restaurants, hotels, offices. Today it barely resembles the open spaces of fifty years ago. Little or no farming remains in the Township. That way of life has disappeared. Instead, an International Airport is within sight and jet planes lazily cruise over the horizon making their approach to the runway.

The emerging industries of coal mining and oil drilling introduced new trades and business activity into the community in the late 1800's. Union Church would profit financially. The Church had purchased six contiguous acres in 1876 for $3,900, and sold the coal beneath for $1,179.20. Later, in 1924, the remainder of the property was sold for $10,000. What a nice profit, $7,279.00, for Union in those hard-scrabble days!

Oil wells were conspicuous and bobbing with regularity around the Church. Old photographs portray derricks on Church property. Session minutes of February 4, 1898, note "the pumping of the Parsonage lot oil well on Sabbath night". In December 1898 council was taken with Attorney Yost in regard to the matter. "If the well was pumped again by the owner on the Lord's day the Congregation would prosecute the owner." Nevertheless, the Church reaped profits from sale of oil, $12,869.74, which helped to defray the cost of our present building.

We have experienced unprecedented progress over 200 years. Technology has given us television, computers, atomic energy, electricity—far too many things for us to enumerate. God has worked through man to achieve these twentieth century miracles. He is truly Lord of History. His power and presence is constant and unchanging. We know progress will not cease as we forge ahead with a sense of frustration and uncertainty into another century.

Union Church will stand like a beacon on our special hill reaching out to the community and to the world. Our local programs strive to address the spiritual needs of our communicants and our neighbors, to provide a caring climate for children, to offer dynamic activities for our youth, to reach out to those in need and to the business community. We never lose sight of our missionary effort throughout the world. As the Presbyterian Church U.S.A. struggles with social problems in this ever-changing society, the motto of the old United Presbyterian Church of which we were a part for 100 years, "The Truth of God—Forbearance in Love" should serve us well.

Church congregation, Sanctuary—1993 Bicentennial. (Photo by Zaccone)

Church congregation, overflow—1993 Bicentennial. (Photo by Zaccone)

Appendices

A. Ministers from Union Church
B. Daughter Churches
C. Missionaries from Union Church
D. Union National Shrine
E. Church Officers (1794-1993)

Appendix A
Ministers from Union Church

The Reverend Joseph K. Riddle
The Reverend James Grier, D.D.
The Reverend Henry C. McFarland
The Reverend George C. Arnold
The Reverend Samuel E. McKee
The Reverend Lafayette Marks
The Reverend George A. B. Robinson
The Reverend William C. Neely
The Reverend John C. Young
The Reverend Samuel J. Glass
The Reverend Andrew W. Verner
The Reverend Jonathan S. Phillips
The Reverend William S. Glass
The Reverend William M. Hendricks
The Reverend James Deemer
The Reverend Michael Holmes
The Reverend Kenneth Anderson
The Reverend Janet Noble
Bruce Ballentine, Seminary Student 1993

Appendix B
Daughter Congregations

Mount Gilead United Presbyterian Church
    Organized June 27, 1843
        This congregation, after many years of good work, was disbanded.

Carnegie United Presbyterian Church
    Organized September 21, 1886

Coraopolis United Presbyterian Church
    Organized September 21, 1886

Ingram United Presbyterian Church
    Organized September 20, 1887

Oakdale United Presbyterian Church
    Organized August 8, 1889

Moon Run United Presbyterian Church
    Organized June 7, 1929

Appendix C
Missionaries from Union Church

Union Congregation is very proud to have had representatives in the foreign Mission Field. Alice Bell Phillips, daughter of Samuel and Alice Scott Phillips, married the Reverend Willard Acheson in 1912 after he graduated from the Pittsburgh Theological Seminary. In August 1913, they sailed to Egypt as Missionaries of the United Presbyterian Church. They spent some time in Assrit and Luxor but most of their work was in Cairo. They returned to America in 1939 because of the Reverend Acheson's ill health. After rest and medical treatment the Reverend Acheson was able to be pastor of the Bolivar, Pennsylvania congregation. In 1945, they returned to Cairo, Egypt where they served until their retirement in June 1952. After several church related jobs, they retired to New Wilmington, PA.

Lois McCurdy, daughter of Elder Joseph McCurdy and Eva M. Aiken McCurdy, married the Reverend Donald Phillips. From 1954 to 1963 they served as missionaries on the island of Luzon in the Philippines. After returning to the states, Rev. Phillips served as pastor of the Linwood Presbyterian Church in Kansas City, MO for 4 years. They are now retired and live in Zelienople, PA.

James Deemer, son of Jerry and Florence Deemer, entered Pittsburgh-Xenia Theological Seminary in 1948 for 2 years. He and his wife, Marian, then entered the mission field in the Sudan for 3 years. They returned in 1953 and Jim returned to the Seminary and was graduated on May 13, 1954. He was ordained into the mission field at Union Church and returned to the Sudan in August 1954. He was assigned to the Boys Secondary School in Omdurman. They returned to the states in 1964 when their son became ill. From 1965 to 1972 he was pastor of the 1st United Presbyterian Church in Long Beach, California. In 1972 he worked for the Inner City Ministries. He passed away June 22, 1986.

Union National Shrine Cemetery.

Appendix D
Union National Shrine

According to the custom of the day, the land surrounding Union Church was consecrated as the resting place of the dead of the Congregation and community. Among the first to be buried within its precincts were soldiers of the American Revolution. This fact automatically brought the Cemetery to the attention of the Pennsylvania Society of National Shrines of the American Revolution which had been founded by patriots in 1775. This Society is an organization of American Community Patriotic Association, consecrated to service to the nation, especially in the preservation of the shrines of the American Revolution, where sleep in eternal glory the revered founders of the American Republic. The burial here of the heroes of the succeeding wars of the nation has tended further to enhance the standing of the Cemetery in the minds and hearts of the National Leaders.

From the date of its founding in 1794, the Cemetery has been under the care of the Fort Turner Shrine Association of Allegheny County. On May 12, 1936, the Ft. Turner Association sent a petition through the Pennsylvania Society to the National Commissioners of the Federation of National Shrines, requesting recognition as a National Shrine. As its contents may be of interest to show what is meant by a National Shrine, part of that petition reads as follows: "That the Local Shrine center at Union United Presbyterian Church, which we have decorated for many years, is, in our judgment the proper place for a National Shrine Ceremonial and Patriotic Meeting. It has within its hallowed precincts the sacred remains of our Founding Fathers, and other distinguished solders and patriots. It is unique, also, in its ancient Indian Traditions.

This place, so qualified, is a region with a great industrial population of New Americans of those foreign stocks who need leadership in Patriotism. We petition that we may have the co-operation of the National Leadership to be constituted a National Shrine.

The petition was filed, and a study made of the facts cited. The leadership of the Ft. Turner Association was examined to determine whether it was equal to the task and free from dangerous radicals who might harm the enterprise. It was approved and plans for the Installation were made. In the presence of a large and distinguished gathering of local and national patriotic leaders and organizations Union National Shrine was constituted on May 12, 1939. The spirit of that meeting has been evident in each recurring annual gathering, as one of complete cooperation, devotion and understanding on the part of all those engaged in this work. The Committee in charge of that meeting consisted of John C. McMichael, Chairman; Lyda Gray, Secretary; Charles Scott, Howard Phillips, W. Alvin McCormick, Mrs. Ruth McCoy Scott, Etta McCormick, Paul G. Volk and Thomas C. McDonough. The Rev. Frank C. Davidson, pastor of the church, was associate chairman. Four Commissioners of the Federation of National Shrines from other states were also present.

It is the thoughtful testimony of local and state leaders of the National Shrine Association that Union Cemetery and Church constitute one of the most logical and beautiful Shrines in the State and in the Nation. Other Shrines may boast a larger number of patriot dead, but considering its frontier nature, its purely rural setting, its nearness to Fort Pitt and surrounding defenses and the fact that the hill upon which the Church is located was for centuries a Beacon of the Indian Tribes inhabiting this locality. Union National Shrine is one of the most important in the State Association. May it never cease to exert an ever increasing influence for good upon the whole community and even upon the nation at large. The local Committee and Pastor attribute to Edward McKee Golden, President of the Pennsylvania Society, National Shrines of the American Revolution, a large share of the success of the Annual Patriotic Assemblies.

THE WAR OF 1776

Moses Ewing	William McCoy	John Phillips
Samuel Dickinson, Sr.	Hugh McCurdy	Jonathan Phillips
Isaac Glass	John McFadden	Joseph Porter
John Hall	Robert McFarland	Samuel Scott
William Hall Sr.	Isaac McMichael	Andrew Spear
John Lorain	John McMichael	Thomas Thornburg
William Marks	Thomas McMillen	Gabriel Walker
John McCoy	John Nickel	Isaac Walker

Appendix

The War of 1812

James Nickel

The War of 1861

James P. Andrews	E. King McCoy	John Scott
John Cooper	William McClaran	Theobald Shaffer
Samuel Eggleson	Newton McCormick	Andrew J. Starrett
John Eggleson	James McMunn	William Stewart
John W. Flowers	William Nickel	E. Watson
William Hall, Jr.	Hugh Nickel	Thomas Williams
Archibald Moore	John M. Phillips	John Young
Charles T. Moore	William Quinn	William H. Young
Samuel McCoy	George K. Sampson	D. C. W. Young

The War of 1917

Howard Andrews	Clyde Mortimer	Merle Schrecengost
Stewart Cummins	Earl Pritchard	Edward Scott

The Honor Roll of the War of 1917, commonly called the First World War; besides those who sleep in Union Shrine, consists of the following:

Wm. M. Boyle, Jr.	John K. Lowry	Claire H. Mortimer
A. Frank Campbell	James C. McLean	Philip Petrie
J. Wm. Campbell	John C. McMichael, Jr	Robert W. Schafer
Gregg Cook	Fred McVey	James H. Scott
James D. Dickson	Hugh M. Maize	Luther Stone
Samuel Fife	K. Noble Maize	George Taylor
Frank Gray	J. Charles Mortimer	James P. Tidball
George Hartman		Dalton W. Verner

The War of 1941

The Honor Roll of the War of 1941, commonly called The War of Liberation, comprise the following, as of October 1, 1944:

Ronald L. Aiken	Robert A. Becker	Gregg W. Cook, Jr.
Robert H. Andrews	Roger E. Boak	Glen W. Corbett

Charles E. Davidson
Frank C. Davidson, Jr.
Robert S. Davidson
Arthur W. Deemer
James R. Deemer
Jerry Davis Deemer, Jr
Chas. W. Dolence
John E. English
Joseph L. English
Ralph L. English
William English
Leonard Frank
James S. Gibb
Richard Gibb
William Gibb
Dawson Gregory
Lloyd A. Harbaugh
Wm. Harbaugh
Jack Harper
Clark Hutchison
Harry F. Klinger, Jr.
James D. Langer
John Langer
Wm. F. Langer

Samuel Lloyd
Walter Lloyd
William Lloyd
Kenneth G. Lowery
John H. Malarky
Chas. W. Matchett
John McCausland
Benj. N. McCormick
Wm A McCormick, Jr
Jos. A McCurdy
James J. McGill
Burd McGinness
Frank McKean
William T. McKenzie
Thomas Milles
Idamae Milles
C. J. Minech
Harry F. Noble
John W. Rowe
Wm. H. Scott
Warren W. Scott
Jos. C. Scott
R. Donald Scott

John R. Scott
Albert L. Scott
Wallace Scott, Jr.
Chas M. Schreiner
Lawrence J. Russ
Robt. W. Phillips
Howard F. Phillips
Dorothy J. Noble
Sam'l J. Mitchell
Albert M. Shones
James E. Shones
Everett R. Trahey
William Tidball
Urban Turner
Robt. C. Uffelman
Dalton E. Verner
Norman E. Verner
James N. Wagner
Robert T. Wright
Edward S. Whiteford
Robert A. White
Fred G. Welton
James R. Williams

HONORABLY DISCHARGED

Russell Babson
Edward Bauer

Merle Conley
Ernest McCobb

Lester Phillips
Wilbur Phillips

CADET NURSES

Jane Malarky
Betty Vale

Martha Hamilton
Betty Jean Learish

Union Presbyterian Church

Present members and past members of Union Church - War of 1941:

WORLD WAR II

Lawrence F. Brammer	George Gettemy	Paul Lucht
Matthew Campbell	Edwin K. Headley	Clifford Nelson
Charles A. Christopher	Richard L. Holmes	Robert Pfaub
Bronson A. Cole	Clair Hopper	G. Warren Trautman
Arletta Connor	Stan Jackson	George Wickline
Walter Ecoff	Jane Limbaugh	Stephen Yamber
	Fred W. Limbaugh	

KOREAN WAR

Ray Aleski	Ray Lenz	Charles Salvitti
Kenneth L. Headley	Warren Mawhinney	James H. Scott
Stan Jackson	R. McNavish	

VIETNAM WAR

Norman Campbell	Harry Phillips	John Trinkala
Tom Connell	Glen R. Sparbanie	Gary Wagner
Michael G. Connor	Donald Tidball	Robert Winning
Daniel J. Nekos		

DESERT STORM CONFLICT

Don Hall	Scott Lucht	Scott McKenzie

CEMETERY

The preceding article has told you that Union Church Cemetery is now a National Shrine. It is with great pride that an interest group gathers each Memorial Day and on National Shrine Day to honor our military dead.

In addition to these, down there in "God's Acre" repose great parents, fathers and mothers, brothers and sisters, husbands and wives and many others of precious memories, who, in years gone by, adorned not only their own homes and firesides but also made this their beloved church home.

There also sleep many who were in no way connected with this congregation. Following are the names of those persons who have been buried in this cemetery in the years gone by.

UNION CEMETERY ASSOCIATION

Union Cemetery Association of Robinson Township was incorporated as a Pennsylvania nonprofit corporation on March 5, 1973. Shortly thereafter it took title to the Union Cemetery property and created a perpetual care fund which has increased each year since inception. Any person who owns a lot in Union Cemetery (or is the oldest direct descendant of a deceased owner) and any person who contributes $100 to the perpetual care fund is a member of Union Cemetery Association.

Union Cemetery Association was founded at the instance of John S. McCormick and others concerned for the improvement and perpetual care of Union Cemetery. The founding trustees of the Association were R. Donald Scott, James Gibb, Nancy Kintz, Charles S. Boyd, Dorothy Davis Reisinger, Elizabeth Lanigan, Anna Pritchard, James H. Scott, and Robert B. Williams. James Wagner, Doris Harper, Clyde English, Darlene Tidball and Jacob H. Phillips, Jr. have also served as Trustees and officers. R. Donald Scott has faithfully served as President of the Association since inception and has also faithfully performed the mowing and maintenance of the Cemetery. Dorothy Wilson has also served the Cemetery faithfully in the sale of lots and the preparation for funerals.

Union Presbyterian Church

The Cemetery Association has been responsible during the past 20 years not only for the day-to-day maintenance of the Cemetery but also for substantial improvements such as the replacement of the stone wall and the erection of the new gate. Other projects have included the laying out of new lots and the meticulous recording of all persons buried in Cemetery for the benefit of posterity.

This list is correct as far as records are obtainable, and current as of June 1, 1993.

CEMETERY

Name	Died	Age	Name	Died	Age
Acheson, Alice Phillips	1980	93	Adams, Lawrence M.	1893	13
Acheson, Joseph Willard	1967	80	Adams, Margaret	1914	73
Ackelson, Birdella	1946	78	Adams, Mary	1849	38
Ackelson, Elizabeth	1871	75	Adams, Mary	1933	
Ackelson, James	1894	64	Adams, Mary G.	1851	38
Ackelson, Jesse W.	1939	73	Adams, Mary M.	1888	6
Ackelson, John	1856	75	Adams, Percy L.	1940	68
Ackelson, Letitia	1910		Adams, Samuel J.	1882	16
Adair, Ann	1903		Adams, Sara J.	1895	73
Adair, Eliza	1908		Adams, Wm.		
Adair, Mary	1833	30	Adams, Wm.	1885	75
Adair, Thomas	1848	21	Adams, Wm.	1912	67
Adair, Wm.	1864	83	Adams (Infant), Mary B.	1890	
Adams, (Infant)	1849		Ahlborn, Elsie	1900	
Adams, Anna L.	1892	67	Ahlborn, Harry	1899	2
Adams, Casper	1915		Aiken, Agnes	1829	67
Adams, Ellen	1926	82	Aiken, Agnes	1870	75
Adams, Elsie May	1888	4	Aiken, Albert	1933	63
Adams, Emma	1913	66	Aiken, Charles J.	1909	30
Adams, J. P.	1883	3	Aiken, Ella	1932	53
Adams, James	1857	45	Aiken, Emma L.	1860	1
Adams, Jane	1888	69	Aiken, Evaline	1905	77
Adams, Jennie M.	1926	79	Aiken, Hannah	1875	17
Adams, John	1926	76	Aiken, Hannah Rose	1925	72

Name	Died	Age	Name	Died	Age
Aiken, Ida	1947	79	Andrews, Wm. J.	1905	47
Aiken, J. Edward	1971	67	Aston, Frederick C.	1941	
Aiken, James	1867	62	Aston, Gertude	1984	100
Aiken, Jessie Moore	1909	39	Aston, Rose Marie	1977	62
Aiken, John	1920	68	Aubrey, Clemence P.	1957	85
Aiken, Jonathan	1892	65	Aubrey, Joseph	1944	80
Aiken, Lillie	1932	68	Aubrey, Joseph	1978	76
Aiken, Mae R.	1917	43	Aubrey, Joseph F.	1973	60
Aiken, Margaret	1901	86	Babson, Horace W.	1949	67
Aiken, Mary Ettie	1870	4	Babson, Katherine	1960	85
Aiken, Sarah M.	1865	65	Badger, Harry	1889	22
Aiken, W. James	1925	63	Baker, Barbara Maria	1959	71
Aiken, Wm.	1911	86	Baker, Elmer J.	1931	
Aiken, Wm. Sr.	1884	77	Baker, Kathlyn	1932	
Aiken, Wm. W.	1903	27	Baker, William	1949	
Albert, Helen	1979	68	Baldwin, Hannah	1789	
Alexander, (Infant)	1939		Bane, (Infant)	1914	
Alexander, (Infant)	1944		Bane, Edna K.	1990	78
Alexander, James	1935	46	Bane, Elwood H.	1970	65
Alexander, Marion	1966	70	Bane, Florence V.	1941	
Alexander, Robert	1967	54	Bane, Hiram Elwood	1954	76
Alexander, Robert James	1936	3	Bane, James Herbert	1965	58
Allen, Sally L.	1990	48	Bane, Leona D.	1975	64
Allison, Merle	1961	62	Barron, Ann J.	1849	25
Allison, Ruth H.	1986	86	Barton, (Infant girl)	1947	
Andrews, Anna M.B.	1930	78	Barton, Charles	1933	
Andrews, Bertha M.	1975	84	Barton, Fredrick J.	1982	80
Andrews, Elizabeth	1861	67	Barton, Fredrick Sr.	1954	75
Andrews, Frank Leo	1951		Barton, Kate	1945	67
Andrews, Howard R.	1942		Barton, Lillian B.	1943	
Andrews, James P.	1867	35	Barton, Mary Louise	1929	
Andrews, Joseph P.	1893	53	Barton, Philip	1927	
Andrews, Mark	1901		Barton, Richard	1933	
Andrews, Mark C.	1923	63	Barwell, George	1918	
Andrews, Mary	1902		Barwell, Mrs.	1918	
Andrews, Samuel	1915	68	Bear, Elmer	1909	
Andrews, Tillie	1924		Beatty, James	1928	76
Andrews, Wm.			Beck, Mr.	1916	

Appendix

Name	Died	Age
Beck, Mrs.	1917	
Bell, Anna Adams	1909	54
Bell, Eliza Jane	1913	68
Bell, J. Hays	1927	78
Bell, James W.	1918	94
Bell, Laura A.	1940	58
Bell, Mary Davis	1931	
Bell, Nelson E.	1929	
Bell, Orlando C.	1909	77
Bender, Ruth R.	1987	71
Betes, A. G.	1922	
Betts, Adam	1908	
Betts, Isabelle	1955	
Betz, Lizzie	1878	6 mo.
Birrough, France Rose	1938	1
Bishop, Joseph	1978	70
Bitenow, Gladys	1915	
Blakely, Mary	1832	11
Blakely, Samuel C.	1853	70
Blakely, Sophia	1832	1
Blyton, (Infant)	1935	
Blyton, John	1932	
Bohn, William G.	1950	
Boisen, Rita L.	1976	69
Boisen, William D.	1969	63
Bolland, John	1959	50
Bolland, Margaret	1950	63
Bonner, Wm.	1830	25
Booth, James	1944	
Booth, Mary M.	1933	
Bowman, Christ	1860	59
Bowman, Maria	1888	86
Boice, David	1856	1
Boice, Jane	1857	36
Boice, John M.	1855	10 mo.
Boice, Nancy Jane	1849	1
Boice, Priscilla	1855	58
Boice, Robert	1860	34

Name	Died	Age
Boice, Samuel	1858	1
Boyd, Gertrude H.	1974	88
Boyd, Richard	1962	48
Boyle, Bert E.	1983	54
Boyle, Bertha M.	1968	63
Boyle, Edward F.	1960	62
Boyle, Richard F.	1983	58
Bracker, August	1918	73
Bracker, Minnie	1925	75
Bracker, Minnie	1956	75
Brammer, Lawrence F.	1984	84
Brammer, Helen M.	1993	79
Briceland, Rev. James	1943	67
Briggs, Margaret	1986	73
Briggs, Robert E.	1978	65
Brimm, Daniel	1903	73
Brimm, Dorothea	1924	92
Brimm, Frederick	1941	
Brimm, Henry W.	1901	27
Brimm, Martha J.	1934	
Britton, Robert J.	1978	54
Brown, Emeline	1864	33
Brown, Hugh	1870	58
Brown, James	1912	
Brown, John S.	1968	63
Brown, Margaret	1876	
Brown, Margaret G.	1984	77
Brown, Mary	1867	34
Brown, Mr.	1905	
Brown, Samuel	1921	
Brown, Wm. K.	1857	8
Brownish, (Infant)	1921	
Brownish, Cain	1921	
Brug, Emil	1968	75
Brug, Emma Frances	1973	79
Brug, William	1977	86
Burg, Ailene Ruth Taylor	1941	
Burianek, Frank	1961	65

Name	Died	Age	Name	Died	Age
Burianek, Johnanna	1947	76	Campbell, H. L.	1918	
Burianek, Joseph Jr.	1982	73	Campbell, Harry V.	1942	
Burianek, Rosetta	1970	75	Campbell, Isabella	1918	87
Burroughs, Archie	1950		Campbell, John J.	1962	83
Burrows		Infant	Campbell, John W.	1957	86
Burrows	1908	Infant	Campbell, Margaret D.	1971	88
Burrows, Agnes	1928	59	Campbell, Matthew	1985	72
Burrows, Ann	1899	75	Campbell, Mrs.	1918	
Burrows, Anna Sheldon	1944	70	Campbell, Norman E.	1984	76
Burrows, Charles Moss	1942	81	Campbell, Sarah A.	1943	
Burrows, Chauncey	1960	59	Cantwell, H. M.	1914	
Burrows, Frank M.	1946	73	Carson, Rebecca	1889	74
Burrows, Hugh	1946	82	Carten, Myrtle Bell	1936	47
Burrows, John C.	1888	76	Cernget	1915	(Infant)
Burrows, Kate	1919	53	Chapman, Donald H.	1960	30
Burrows, Mary	1880	2	Chapman, Ernst L.	1976	62
Burrows, Mary Ann	1931	91	Chapman, George H.	1967	74
Burrows, Wm. W.	1920	90	Chapman, James	1946	56
Burrows, Wm. W.	1940	73	Chapman, James S.	1937	
Butler, William John	1955	43	Chapman, Jennie M.	1963	68
Byers, James G.	1945	80	Chapman, Mary Ellen	1935	70
Caldwell, Agnes A.	1864	31	Chapman, Nellie C.	1949	56
Caldwell, Ella A.	1858	60	Chapman, Stella E.	1985	69
Caldwell, George M.	1897	65	Charleston, Annie	1882	65
Caldwell, Hannah M.	1864	24	Charleston, Joseph	1890	75
Caldwell, Lettie McC.	1895	67	Chess, Alexander	1948	57
Caldwell, William	1870	70	Chess, Andrew	1929	67
Caldwell, William A.	1853	24	Chess, Annie	1979	85
Campbell	1918	(Infant)	Chess, Labine	1926	66
Campbell, Alex	1977	51	Clapperton, Anna	1955	74
Campbell, Annie	1914		Clapperton, James	1986	78
Campbell, Charles E.	1983	84	Clapperton, John	1944	
Campbell, Daisy	1918		Clark, Helen M.	1956	52
Campbell, Edith	1915		Clark, William	1957	56
Campbell, Elizabeth	1897	54	Cochenour, Margaret	1989	68
Campbell, Emma Cora	1953	80	Cole, Bronson	1982	66
Campbell, Freda	1993	80	Cooke, James	1859	68
Campbell, Guy	1940		Cooper, Hugh Lee	1931	

Appendix

Name	Died	Age	Name	Died	Age
Cooper, John	1863	33	Dickson, Andrew Howard	1884	23
Corbett, Glenn	1944	19	Dickson, Andrew W.	1872	23
Corbett, Isabelle	1975	74	Dickson, J. Herbert	1917	32
Cowan, Hannah			Dickson, Joseph M.	1915	75
Cowan, Harry	1900		Dickson, Lettitie	1866	55
Cowan, Harry	1909		Dickson, M. James	1926	72
Cowan, Henry			Dickson, Mary	1934	88
Cowan, Hugh	1861	74	Dickson, Porter McB.	1910	23
Cowan, Jane	1850	55	Dickson, Samuel	1915	77
Crozier, Elizabeth	1962	75	Dickson, Samuel	1949	33
Crozier, John	1963	73	Dickson, Samuel Sr.	1838	78
Crum, Howard H.	1982	86	Dickson, Sara Ann	1920	68
Crum, Irene	1959	61	Dickson, Sarah E.	1921	72
Culley, Shirley	1973	34	Dickson, Susannah	1884	72
Cummings, Alexander	1919	59	Dickson, William A.	1843	6 Mo.
Cummings, Georgiacia	1955	87	Dilkes, Charles	1853	20
Cummings, Isabella S.	1929	64	Dilkes, Hugh A.	1862	9 Mo.
Cummings, James	1931		Dlugosz, Janice	1956	10 Mo.
Cummings, James M.	1965	65	Dlugosz, Raymond	1968	20
Cummings, Stewart L.	1920		Dobbin, Ann		
Cummings, Thomas F.	1913	27	Dobbin, John	1854	59
Cushner	1914	(Infant)	Dolence, Emma M.	1955	62
Dalzell, Mary A.	1853	1 Mo.	Dolence, Joseph J.	1969	78
Darnley, James P.	1943	38	Dolence, Violet L.	1966	44
Darnley, William R.	1923		Donahoe, Samuel E.	1991	(Infant)
Davidson, Edith	1972	81	Double, Elmer E.	1944	
Davidson, Frank C.	1946	62	Double, Isabelle F.	1970	72
Davis, Francis W. Sr.	1972	53	Double, John E.	1970	78
Davis, James M.	1856	5 mo.	Double, Leonard P.	1936	20
Davis, Thomas M. Jr.	1956	(Infant)	Double, Louis	1934	3 Mo.
Davis, Victoria	1924		Double, Susan L.	1966	96
Deemer, Florence	1967	69	Double, Walter E.	1956	61
Deemer, Jerry D.	1986	88	Drexler, Charles	1944	78
Deer, Elizabeth	1911	66	Drexler, Frank	1966	74
Deer, John H.	1924	74	Drexler, Janet	1932	
DeVassie, Mary Badger	1939	85	Drexler, John	1920	
DeVassie, William	1928	65	Drexler, Mary	1943	49
Dickson, Andrew	1897	91	Drexler, Ralph	1939	19

Name	Died	Age	Name	Died	Age
Drexler, Raymond E.	1948	24	Ewing, Lillie Gilson	1935	71
Droblitz, Jake	1929		Ewing, Margaret	1845	5
Duff, Mary Jane	1862	27	Ewing, Margaret	1893	87
Duffy, Vincent	1961	66	Ewing, Moses	1815	85
Dyurico, Andie	1938	(Infant)	Ewing, Nelson	1902	82
Eagleson, Kate	1908	71	Ewing, Sophia	1837	69
Eaton, George	1959	57	Ewing, Wilda	1892	42
Eaton, Violet A.	1974	62	Ewing, William	1842	2
Edmundson, Eliza	1911		Ewing, William	1868	81
Edmundson, Elizabeth	1858		Ewing, William	1936	77
Edmundson, Elmer	1882		Fhy, Mary E.	1924	69
Edmundson, Etta	1910		Filadelfia	1931	
Edmundson, Hester A.	1896	70	Filadelfia, Norma J.	1933	
Edmundson, Homer	1858		Fitzpatrick, Linda R.	1988	40
Edmundson, James	1871	42	Flowers, John W.	1926	84
Edmundson, Jennie	1935	70	Forgey, Andrew		
Edmundson, John	1894	71	Forgey, Thomas		
Edmundson, John	1932	73	Forgey, William		
Edmundson, Joseph		70	Fortney, John E.	1983	66
Edmundson, Mary			Frame, Adeline	1918	
Edmundson, Rufus	1856		Frame, George	1919	
Edmundson, Sarah		70	Frame, George	1943	
English, Bernice M.	1987	69	Frame, Johan S.	1967	69
English, William E.	1989	74	Frame, Lena P.	1974	75
Ewing, Ann	1842	4	Frame, Margaret	1942	
Ewing, Annie	1835	12	Frame, Robert	1919	
Ewing, Annie W.	1886	31	Freebing, Valera	1921	
Ewing, Daniel	1880	73	Freebing, William E.	1951	60
Ewing, Elenor	1845	3	Fry, Charles E.	1984	77
Ewing, Elwilda	1906		Fry, Leona S.	1976	64
Ewing, Henry	1851	27	Fullmore, Agnes S.	1921	
Ewing, Issabella	1876	40	Gale	1915	Infant
Ewing, Issaca	1892	81	Garland, James	1919	
Ewing, James	1906	61	Gayup, Frank	1923	
Ewing, James	1925		Gayup, Lawrence	1922	
Ewing, Jane	1852	68	Gayup, Mathew	1926	
Ewing, Jane	1887	68	Gensler, Joseph J.	1987	91
Ewing, Lemon O.	1855	10 Mo.	Gensler, Rosella M.	1972	71

Appendix

Name	Died	Age	Name	Died	Age
Geyser, Albert	1957	86	Glass, Issac	1826	66
Geyser, Anna M.	1955	81	Glass, Jane	1870	78
Geyser, Charles	1940		Glass, Jane Stewart	1849	2
Geyser, E. K.	1917		Glass, Leonard D.	1982	79
Geyser, Fred	1948	79	Glass, Lizzie	1948	70
Geyser, George	1930		Glass, Margaret	1886	4
Geyser, Henry	1921	53	Glass, Margaret Anna	1889	45
Geyser, Jane M.	1953	63	Glass, Margaret J. S.	1852	4
Geyser, John	1931		Glass, Martha M.	1973	87
Geyser, Joseph	1939	75	Glass, Mary	1846	87
Geyser, Joseph	1972	84	Glass, Mary	1864	59
Geyser, Martha	1942		Glass, Nelson	1886	2
Geyser, Martha J.	1950		Glass, Rocsa	1908	55
Geyser, Michael	1942		Glass, Samuel	1891	72
Geyser, Mrs.	1916		Glass, Samuel Sr.	1864	81
Geyser, Mrs.	1916	89	Glass, Samuel J. Jr.	1968	77
Geyser, William	1930		Glass, Samuel James	1943	
Geyser, William C.	1981	95	Glass, Samuel S.	1902	61
Gibb, David	1927	16	Glass, Sara E.	1947	78
Gibb, Jean H.	1971	84	Glass, Sarah McCurdy	1895	79
Gibb, John M.	1977	62	Glass, William	1901	90
Gibb, Thomas	1922	39	Glass, William D.	1984	83
Glass	1907	(Infant)	Glass, William H.	1948	71
Glass	1935	(Infant)	Glass, William S.	1856	9 Mo.
Glass, Albert P.	1933		Glass, Wm. Aiken	1857	6
Glass, Amy Ewing	1935	80	Goater, Elizabeth	1901	
Glass, Andrew D.	1858	2 Mo.	Goater, Francis		
Glass, Clara	1947	62	Gorjup, Gertrude	1952	63
Glass, Dianne M.	1992	52	Gorjup, Rudole	1955	66
Glass, Edward E.	1973	77	Gould, Ann L.	1936	65
Glass, Emma	1932		Goulding, Elizabeth	1894	51
Glass, Etta Marlene	1937		Goulding, John	1910	66
Glass, Eurilda D.	1992	95	Grace, Elizabeth A.	1953	77
Glass, Evaline Jane	1993	94	Grace, Harry	1948	75
Glass, Hannah A.	1963	85	Graham, Elizabeth E.	1852	2
Glass, Hannah Aiken	1897	73	Graham, Jane	1852	42
Glass, Hannah Mary	1853	3	Graham, Mary E.	1853	
Glass, Irene	1875	35	Grames, Miss	1906	

Name	Died	Age	Name	Died	Age
Gribben, Abigal	1830	20	Harbinson		Infant
Gribben, Esther	1851	40	Harbinson, Alice		
Gribben, Esther A.	1851	2	Harbinson, Jane	1855	43
Gribben, Oliver P.	1846	3	Harbinson, Matthew	1853	73
Grier, Jane	1849	78	Harbinson, Mrs.		
Grier, Joseph	1884	79	Harbinson, William H.	1951	
Grier, Margaret J.	1854	37	Harper	1914	Infant
Grier, Minnie			Harper, George C.	1982	95
Grier, Nathan	1842	75	Harper, Jack W.	1978	59
Guiser, Michael	1893	71	Harper, Lyda R.	1976	91
Gyory	1941	Infant	Harrower, Robert	1944	78
Hale, Robert H.	1985	46	Harrower, Elizabeth M.	1947	83
Hall, Ann	1840	80	Harrower, Norma	1928	24
Hall, Jane		94	Hartig, August	1929	
Hall, John	1829	76	Hartig, Harry	1921	
Hall, John	1845	19	Hartig, Martha	1924	
Hall, Lettie	1836	74	Harton, John	1922	
Hall, Lettie	1857		Hasting, Elmer G.	1922	
Hall, Matthew	1817	27	Heckele, Amy	1956	69
Hall, Samuel	1860		Heckele, John	1947	73
Hall, Sarah A.	1865	35	Heckle, Elizabeth F.	1936	87
Hall, William Jr.	1878	31	Heimburg, Charles F.	1990	68
Hall, William Sr.	1819	68	Hicks, Paul J. Jr.	1982	49
Hall, William Sr.	1870	75	Hiles, Ruth	1951	45
Hamilton, Adelene	1932		Hiles, Samuel Kay	1930	
Hamilton, Alex	1837	27	Hill	1888	Infant
Hamilton, Margaret	1838	49	Hill, Anna T.	1962	73
Hamilton, Mary Jane	1835	16	Hill, Edna E.	1934	32
Hamilton, Sarah	1837	24	Hill, Elizabeth DeVassie	1958	92
Harbaugh	1915	Infant	Hill, Wickfield D.	1897	13
Harbaugh, Bertha	1928	29	Hillburg, William	1908	
Harbaugh, Clyde	1953	53	Holland, Simon	1926	
Harbaugh, Ellen	1922	70	Holmes, Bertha W.	1892	8
Harbaugh, G. Lewis	1959	84	Holmes, Edna M.	1976	87
Harbaugh, Harvey R.	1969	71	Holmes, Hannah F.	1891	37
Harbaugh, James E.	1959	32	Holmes, John F. S.	1892	4
Harbaugh, Lorene	1915	36	Holmes, John H. W.	1887	8
Harbaugh, Marie B.	1964	57	Holmes, Maria L.		8 Mo.

Appendix 109

Name	Died	Age	Name	Died	Age
Holmes, Mary Jane	1942	24	Jones, Margaret N.	1940	
Holmes, Mrs.	1912		Jones, Mrs.	1908	
Holmes, Richard L.	1976	51	Jones, Nathan	1949	87
Holmes, Sadie C.	1942		Kanuck, Steve J.	1982	71
Holmes, William F.	1969	88	Kanyuck, Andrew	1949	58
Holmes, William Karl	1976	63	Kanyuck, Elizabeth O.	1948	56
Holmes, William T.	1882	8	Kearnes, Mary	1918	
Holt, Barry A.	1982	31	Kearns, Evelyn A.	1979	76
Hopper, Clara Y.	1981	77	Kearns, Uriah B.	1971	69
Hopper, Hannah Jane	1965	85	Keating, Isaac		67
Hopper, Joseph	1944	67	Keating, Margaret	1852	72
Hopper, Mary	1923	75	Kelley, Albert M.	1943	
Hopper, Samuel E.	1960	83	Kelley, Alice G.	1964	91
Hopper, William E.	1990	88	Kelley, Elizabeth	1855	30
Hopper, William J.	1904	58	Kells, John H. M.	1890	1 month
Hopson	1915	Infant	Kelso	1935	(Infant)
Hunter, Anna L.	1938	78	Kelso, Eliza		
Hunter, George	1914	27	Kelso, Fannie		
Hunter, James	1911		Kelso, George W.	1917	44
Ihrig, Lucy	1986	88	Kelso, Howard E.	1990	77
Ihrig, Theodore E.	1962	76	Kelso, James		
Innes, Ida Mary Huss	1938	80	Kelso, James C.	1927	58
Innes, John C.	1935	75	Kelso, Jane		
Innes, Wilson J.	1940		Kelso, John C.	1869	27
Irvin	1939	Infant	Kelso, Katherine	1881	60
Irvine, James A.	1957	65	Kelso, Louise	1906	61
Irvine, Lena E.	1981	74	Kelso, Lucinda		
Irwin, James			Kelso, Mary E.		
Irwin, John			Kelso, Sarah J.	1973	91
Irwin, Mary			Kelso, William E.	1881	50
Jackson, Paige M.	1990	10 Mo.	Kelso, William G.	1929	20
James, Ida Mary	1922	61	Kerkwood, Mary Bell	1928	
Jenkins, Edward	1912		Kerkwood, Roy	1917	
Jenkins, John	1918	36	Kerr, Dale A.	1987	80
Jenkins, Samuel	1915	74	Kerr, Daniel	1839	30
Jewett, Floris	1896		Kerr, Mary	1855	80
Jones, Dr.	1939		Kerr, Mary Jane	1869	
Jones, Laura McCurdy	1909	52	Kerr, Sarah	1891	

Appendix

Name	Died	Age	Name	Died	Age
Kerwood, Elizabeth O.	1936	72	Link, Grace Adams	1930	58
Kinney, Margaret E.	1972	65	Linton		Infant
Kirkwood, Harry	1948		Linton, Della		
Kirrmann, Dorothy J.	1966	73	Linton, James	1894	62
Klinger, Harry F.	1980	62	Linton, James	1921	22
Klinger, Harry Frederick III	1943	Infant	Linton, Martha J.	1984	80
Koffer, Joseph	1944		Linton, Mary B.	1945	82
Kozuiki, Mary	1935	45	Linton, Robert		
Kriss, Andrew	1982	81	Linton, Samuel		70
Kuzemka, Harry Sr.	1959	72	Linton, Samuel	1940	76
Langer, Edward	1929	56	Linton, Sarah		69
Langer, Eva	1934	83	Linton, Sarah	1873	32
Langer, Frank	1969	86	Lister, Elsie M.	1991	70
Langer, George Sr.	1965	71	Lloyd, William N.	1991	81
Langer, Jacob	1964	84	Lloyd, Frank	1981	75
Langer, John	1922	82	Lobritz, Frances	1939	67
Langer, John	1931		Lobritz, John	1946	66
Langer, Kathryn	1967	74	Logan, Jane	1855	68
Langer, William	1953	81	Logan, John	1847	65
Larimer, Sara F.	1939		Logan, John	1848	67
LaRoss, Laura A.	1970	85	Logan, John	1917	
Lawver, Gertrude M.	1989	81	Logan, John	1921	
Leap, Mary M.	1992	77	Logan, John H.	1852	2
Learish, David E.	1984	87	Logan, John S.	1824	7 Mo.
Learish, Laura	1973	76	Logan, Mary	1849	66
Legget, Mrs.	1905		Logan, Robert	1839	60
Leopold, Jacob	1931		Logan, Samuel	1873	Infant
Lescallette, Mary J.	1991	95	Logan, Sarah Ann	1899	
Lescallette, Richard F.	1970	71	Logan, Sarah M.	1844	20
Lescallette, Richard S.	1973	47	Logan, Stewart	1907	
Lesley, Thomas	1822	50	Lorain, Elizabeth		
Liesch, Grant H.	1976	59	Lorain, Elizabeth		
Liggett		Infant	Lorain, Elizabeth	1821	4 Mo.
Liggett, Eleanor	1870	32	Lorain, John	1834	79
Liggett, Ida E.	1870	2	Lorain, Mary		
Limbaugh, Jane	1989	68	Lorain, Mary	1814	48
Lindsey, Nancy		37	Lorain, Parker	1862	70
Link, George C.	1922	62	Lowery, Verna Scott	1923	25

Appendix

Name	Died	Age
Lowrey, Elizabeth E.	1965	74
Lowrey, John K.	1974	83
Lowrey, Kenneth G.	1980	56
Lowril, Mae F.	1932	
Lubic, Albert J.	1963	59
Lubic, Linda L.	1977	45
Lubic, Mae I.	1984	79
Macek, Matthew	1990	83
Markham	1921	Infant
Markham, John	1929	
Marks, D. M.	1850	35
Marks, Elizabeth	1824	73
Marks, Elizabeth	1855	81
Marks, Jacob H.	1828	14
Marks, Joseph F.	1850	
Marks, Sarah	1851	27
Marks, William		
Marks, William Sr.	1824	73
Marshall, Archibald J.	1942	
Marshall, Elizabeth B.	1944	77
Marsico, Emily S.	1979	50
Martin, Andrew J.	1959	88
Martin, Anna	1984	67
Martin, Jannette	1965	86
Martin, Valentine W.	1945	37
Martino, Elanor M.	1951	29
Mastin, Lester Homer	1940	
Matthew, Noble H.	1990	64
McAlister, James		
McAlister, Mary	1862	72
McBride, Jean McClarim	1943	
McCalinus, Mrs	1918	
McCandless, Ida E.	1919	60
McCartney, Mabel B.	1992	93
McCartney, Mildred E.	1990	62
McCartney, William	1959	63
McCauley, Lelah	1946	55
McClain, Daniel	1924	
McClarren		Infant
McClarren, Diana	1896	73
McClarren, Elizabeth	1921	
McClarren, Sarah		
McClarren, Wm.	1913	
McClarren, Wm. Sr.	1893	81
McClelland, Emanda J.	1908	61
McClelland, Emily L.	1880	74
McClelland, John	1894	84
McCloskey		
McCloskey, Elizabeth	1857	58
McCloskey, Henry	1880	42
McCloskey, Hiram		
McCloskey, John Esq.	1879	81
McCluskey, Cyrus	1895	70
McCluskey, Rachel	1893	79
McConnell, Mary L.	1945	54
McCormick		Infant
McCormick, Andrew J.	1840	1
McCormick, Benj. Frank	1889	8
McCormick, Benj. Newton	1939	98
McCormick, Benjamin	1888	76
McCormick, Eleanor	1895	90
McCormick, Elizabeth	1861	77
McCormick, Elsie	1988	96
McCormick, Etta R.	1961	77
McCormick, Helen L.	1990	68
McCormick, Hugh	1852	86
McCormick, Hugh	1894	80
McCormick, Hugh	1894	80
McCormick, James E.		
McCormick, John W.	1854	37
McCormick, Joseph L.	1896	46
McCormick, Letitia G.	1905	54
McCormick, Margaret	1854	75
McCormick, Richard	1895	50
McCormick, William	1875	83
McCormick, William A. Jr.	1984	62

Name	Died	Age	Name	Died	Age
McCormick, William A. Sr.	1968	85	McCurdy, Andrew	1840	55
McCoy		Infant	McCurdy, Andrew	1849	1
McCoy, Alexander	1855	23	McCurdy, Andrew	1933	
McCoy, Alexander	1871	52	McCurdy, Dorothy Evelyn	1938	12
McCoy, Amanda	1851	3 Mo.	McCurdy, Eliza	1814	3
McCoy, Amelia	1849	20	McCurdy, Elizabeth	1828	3
McCoy, David C.	1854	17	McCurdy, Elizabeth	1829	40
McCoy, Elijah	1856	16	McCurdy, Elizabeth	1838	30
McCoy, Elizabeth	1856	54	McCurdy, Elmer		
McCoy, Elizabeth	1881	84	McCurdy, Eva M.	1976	83
McCoy, Elizabeth	1897	95	McCurdy, Florence R.	1959	95
McCoy, Esbella	1927	87	McCurdy, Frank	1929	
McCoy, Ethel	1963	82	McCurdy, George W.	1958	86
McCoy, Hannah	1855	53	McCurdy, Grizzila		
McCoy, James	1869	82	McCurdy, Hugh		
McCoy, James W.	1965	53	McCurdy, Hugh	1843	33
McCoy, Jane	1849	5	McCurdy, Jane C.	1845	41
McCoy, Jane	1904	76	McCurdy, Joseph	1825	37
McCoy, John	1861	40	McCurdy, Joseph	1848	26
McCoy, John Jr.	1846	18	McCurdy, Joseph	1910	86
McCoy, John Sr.	1820	59	McCurdy, Joseph D.	1982	90
McCoy, Lillie M.	1935	57	McCurdy, Kate	1914	55
McCoy, Mary A.	1878	66	McCurdy, Margaret A.	1824	5
McCoy, Robert	1858	26	McCurdy, Mary	1833	15
McCoy, Sadie J.	1879	8 Mo.	McCurdy, Mary	1857	69
McCoy, Samuel	1862	27	McCurdy, Mary	1882	68
McCoy, Samuel	1872		McCurdy, Mary A.	1913	82
McCoy, Sarah	1831	60	McCurdy, Rebecca	1852	50
McCoy, Sarah K.	1906	83	McCurdy, Samuel	1857	58
McCoy, Thomas	1850	42	McCutcheon, John	1957	83
McCoy, Thomas	1922	81	McCutcheon, Margaret	1935	
McCoy, Thomas W.	1963	81	McElherron, Margaret	1854	28
McCoy, William	1820	62	McElherron, William K.	1872	18
McCoy, William	1842		McFadden, Carrie	1864	10
McCoy, William	1882	85	McFadden, John	1849	10
McCoy, William J.	1961	84	McFadden, John Jr.	1870	70
McCurdy, Alexander	1861	31	McFadden, John Sr.	1836	70
McCurdy, Andrew			McFadden, Mary	1850	86

Appendix 113

Name	Died	Age	Name	Died	Age
McFadden, Rachel	1873	63	McKenzie, Anna	1929	93
McFadden, Samuel M.C.	1845	7 Mo.	McKenzie, Bertha B.	1925	48
McFarland, Alexander	1872	90	McKenzie, James	1904	72
McFarland, Andrew B.	1873	49	McKenzie, Thomas A.	1939	80
McFarland, Eleaner	1867	51	McKnight, James	1850	78
McFarland, James	1882	74	McKnight, James M.	1954	68
McFarland, Margaret	1854	66	McKnight, Margaret M.	1983	92
McFarland, Margaret	1896	84	Buried in Scotland		
McFarland, Margaret (Fields)	1866	27	McKowan, Hannah L.	1946	80
McFarland, Mary	1844	30	McKown, James C.	1926	66
McFarland, Robert	1824	99	McLean, Anna	1936	83
McFarland, Robert	1899	69	McMichael, Ann	1845	45
McFarland, Sarah	1889	70	McMichael, Anna V.	1957	78
McFarland, William	1896	67	McMichael, Cecile M.	1969	60
McGaray, Naomi Diana	1936		McMichael, Clarence	1896	19
McGarr, Jane T.	1908	70	McMichael, Elanor	1869	59
McGeary, Thomas D.	1957	Infant	McMichael, Ella	1931	
McGill, Andrew	1962	71	McMichael, Hanna	1863	19
McGill, Susan	1981	84	McMichael, Howard R.	1953	60
McGinness, James	1877	36	McMichael, Isaac	1823	67
McGregor, Eliza C.	1891	69	McMichael, Isaac	1862	27
McGregor, Elizabeth	1856	61	McMichael, Isaac	1904	69
McGregor, James	1867	83	McMichael, James S.	1935	68
McGregor, Margaret	1891	68	McMichael, James W.	1873	65
McGregor, Samuel E.			McMichael, Jean	1966	70
McIlvain, Elizabeth	1863	23	McMichael, John	1840	79
McKay, Hoy C.	1937	6 Mo.	McMichael, John	1853	60
McKean, Edith G.	1988	81	McMichael, John	1922	84
McKean, Edna C.	1976	77	McMichael, John C.	1968	73
McKean, Emma F.	1983	81	McMichael, John C.	1987	73
McKean, Joseph	1967	71	McMichael, John Y.	1899	3
McKean, Walter	1967	74	McMichael, Leah E.	1850	52
McKee, Deborah	1887	95	McMichael, Margaret	1863	19
McKee, George	1837	64	McMichael, Margaret	1926	78
McKee, John	1815	13	McMichael, Margaret F.	1964	59
McKee, Margaret	1825	54	McMichael, Mary E.	1857	18
McKee, Nancy	1910	85	McMichael, Mirian	1846	85
McKee, William	1821	21	McMichael, Nancy	1849	77

Name	Died	Age	Name	Died	Age
McMichael, Ralph C.	1962	76	Miller, Howard E.	1961	73
McMichael, Samuel D.	1844	4	Miller, Mary	1807	2
McMichael, Sarah	1870	74	Miller, Nellie	1993	89
McMichael, Stella	1939	57	Miller, Sara G.	1984	84
McMichael, William			Milles, Jane Adams	1920	73
McMichael, William J.	1844	1	Milles, Joseph J.	1908	34
McMillin, Carne	1894	41	Milles, Mae M.	1964	84
McMillin, Carrie	1894		Milles, Thomas E.	1952	68
McMillin, Ebenezer			Minech, Clarence	1959	79
McMillin, Joseph	1852	45	Minech, Mary E.	1969	89
McMillin, Margaret	1898	79	Mischisen, Nicholas	1990	74
McMillin, Margaret	1918	59	Mitchell	1915	
McMillin, Mary	1844	78	Mitchell, Elizabeth	1925	
McMillin, Samuel			Mitchell, H.	1914	
McMillin, Sarah	1926	80	Mitchell, Jacob	1821	1
McMillin, Thomas	1831	76	Mitchell, James	1822	1
McMillin, Thomas	1862	17	Mitchell, John	1845	21
McMillin, William H.	1847	1	Mitchell, Joseph	1920	
McMunn, Samuel			Mitchell, Katherine	1910	
McMunn, Samuel G.			Mitchell, Margaret	1890	94
McMunn, Sarah			Mitchell, Margaret	1926	
McMurray, Clyde	1950		Mitchell, Mary	1846	21
McMurray, Ida	1978	75	Mitchell, Michael	1846	51
McMurray, Robert L.	1963	36	Mitchell, Samuel B.	1893	62
McNeal	1932		Mitchell, Susanna	1831	4
McVay, Charles S.	1896	1	Mitchell, Thomas	1846	32
McVay, Elizabeth	1918	62	Moore		Infant
McVay, Harry	1926	62	Moore, Archbald	1874	34
McVay, Irene J.	1898	1	Moore, Charles	1864	22
Mefford, Fred E.	1959	83	Moore, Charles	1866	66
Mellott, Wiley G.	1990	66	Moore, Eliza J.	1864	27
Mertz, Amanda	1904	66	Moore, Letty J.	1905	76
Mertz, George M.	1900	69	Moore, Margaret	1861	44
Mickliff, P. Hill	1897	13	Moore, Margaret A.	1864	26
Miller, Benjamin	1822	39	Moore, Mary	1865	33
Miller, Carrie M.	1969	75	Moore, Mary J.	1864	20
Miller, Charles A.	1965	76	Moreland, Elizabeth	1829	57
Miller, Elizabeth	1856	55	Morgan, Mary	1814	80

Appendix 115

Name	Died	Age
Morgan, Wm.	1901	
Mortimer, Clare H.	1965	72
Mortimer, Clyde D.	1938	45
Mortimer, Margaret E.	1992	94
Mortimer, Martha E.	1934	
Mortimer, Robert	1921	
Moss, Charles	1901	94
Moss, David E.	1946	91
Moss, Dayton	1924	
Moss, Harold	1923	
Moss, Mary P.	1911	97
Moss, Mary Jane	1915	75
Motherwell, David	1922	
Murdock, James	1886	44
Murdock, Lawrence	1902	16
Myers, Grace	1976	79
Neely, Sallie M.	1876	22
Nelson, Johanna	1944	
Nelson, Louis K.	1904	6
Nelson, May	1929	
Nelson, Peter	1934	
Nelson, Rosella E.	1992	92
Nicily, Martha	1940	88
Nickle, Alexander	1843	13
Nickle, Ann		
Nickle, Ann	1856	41
Nickle, Catharine		
Nickle, Christena	1854	17
Nickle, Elizabeth	1853	63
Nickle, Hugh	1861	60
Nickle, James		
Nickle, John	1807	
Nickle, John	1854	66
Nickle, John	1881	62
Nickle, Martha M.	1840	8
Nickle, Sarah	1863	56
Nickle, William J.		
Nixon, Edward G.	1965	63

Name	Died	Age
Noah, Lee A.	1961	76
Noble, Ethelyn B.	1986	58
Nolle, Thomas	1946	30
Obenour	1928	Infant
Obenour, Charles E.	1944	22
Obenour, Joseph	1934	50
Obenour, Sarah B.	1960	69
Oberdick, Anthony Louis	1944	
Oberdick, Carolyn	1948	79
Padglek, Adolph	1960	73
Palmer, John	1910	62
Park, Jane F.	1948	59
Park, John	1966	79
Parkinson, Charlotte R.	1986	75
Parkinson, William W.	1967	72
Parks, Annie	1937	52
Patterson, Anastasia	1927	
Patterson, James	1907	
Pearson, Harry A.	1966	84
Peggins, Mary H.	1949	
Peggins, Norman	1951	
Penney, Bessie McCoy	1942	66
Penney, David W.	1971	96
Perkins, Frances	1901	
Pestial, Thomas	1915	
Peters, Edward B.	1990	71
Peterson, August	1923	
Peterson, Mr.	1909	
Phillips		Infant
Phillips	1872	Infant
Phillips	1874	Infant
Phillips	1933	Infant
Phillips, Agnes	1867	15
Phillips, Alexander	1850	46
Phillips, Alexander	1875	51
Phillips, Alexander Jr.	1859	74
Phillips, Alice Scott	1916	58

Name	Died	Age	Name	Died	Age
Phillips, Andrew N.	1944		Phillips, Jonathan	1837	27
Phillips, Ann			Phillips, Jonathan J.	1817	22
Phillips, Ann	1868	49	Phillips, Laura M.	1959	51
Phillips, Anna R.	1976	78	Phillips, M. McC.	1897	82
Phillips, Calvin K.	1950	84	Phillips, Margaret H.	1893	24
Phillips, Clara B.	1957	90	Phillips, Margaret J.	1883	57
Phillips, Edna J.	1982	68	Phillips, Margaret J.	1951	
Phillips, Eliza M.			Phillips, Martha	1841	41
Phillips, Elizabeth	1834	80	Phillips, Mary	1869	83
Phillips, Elizabeth A.	1950		Phillips, Mary D.	1879	10 Mo.
Phillips, Ella Mae	1932		Phillips, Matilda	1859	49
Phillips, Elmo	1955	67	Phillips, Matilda	1897	57
Phillips, Emaline	1902	69	Phillips, Milton S.	1923	71
Phillips, Estella M.	1959	87	Phillips, Priscilla	1867	72
Phillips, Ethel M.	1963	65	Phillips, Priscilla J.	1867	2
Phillips, Fannie E.	1867	10	Phillips, Roy C.	1972	66
Phillips, Frances	1943		Phillips, Samuel	1854	23
Phillips, Frank H.	1963	88	Phillips, Samuel	1863	74
Phillips, Hannah			Phillips, Samuel	1901	63
Phillips, Hannah	1825	70	Phillips, Samuel	1911	61
Phillips, Hannah M.	1857	2 Mo.	Phillips, Samuel B.	1894	85
Phillips, Hannah P.	1858	22	Phillips, Sarah	1895	61
Phillips, Harris	1960	59	Phillips, Susannah	1873	94
Phillips, Harris L.	1979	50	Phillips, Thomas	1902	59
Phillips, Helen	1904	2	Phillips, Thomas Esq.	1853	31
Phillips, Howard S.	1966	81	Phillips, Vesta	1963	59
Phillips, Jacob L.	1992	81	Phillips, William	1971	75
Phillips, James	1879	66	Phillips, William J.	1932	
Phillips, James B.	1910	31	Phillips, William P.	1928	24
Phillips, Jane	1892	78	Phillips, William S	1912	81
Phillips, Jane France	1941		Phillips, William Sr.	1860	73
Phillips, Johathan	1902	82	Pierce, Sarah	1873	69
Phillips, John			Pietred, Thomas	1917	
Phillips, John	1834	84	Pintar, Anthony A.	1958	50
Phillips, John M.	1905	68	Poppinghous, John	1935	76
Phillips, John S.	1867	56	Porigneaux, Eli	1984	62
Phillips, John W.	1929	65	Porter, Amanda	1866	21
Phillips, Jonathan	1830	81	Porter, Jane	1857	80

Appendix 117

Name	Died	Age	Name	Died	Age
Porter, Joseph	1843	29	Rape, Della	1966	88
Porter, Mary	1848	37	Rape, Harry L.	1959	83
Porter, Paul A.	1982	74	Ray, Elizabeth	1870	70
Porter, Robert E.	1872	70	Rea, Aaron	1861	28
Porter, Sarah E.	1869	38	Rea, Henry	1862	32
Potter, Ethel M.	1966	91	Rea, Robert L.	1849	23
Powell, Mattie	1932		Reed	1916	Infant
Powers, Shirley A.	1982	55	Reed	1917	Infant
Price, Annie	1863	1 Mo.	Reed	1919	Infant
Price, John	1922		Reed, Emma R.	1918	56
Price, Mary	1897	78	Rhodes, Annie	1917	
Price, McGowen	1862	1	Richard, Hanna H.	1937	80
Price, Sarah	1873	69	Richard, James H.	1945	90
Price, Sarah J.	1864	1 Mo.	Richards, Paul Jr.	1949	48
Price, William J.	1868	17	Riddle, Emma R.	1953	98
Pritchard, Anna A.	1961	83	Riddle, Hugh	1891	86
Pritchard, Anna A.	1991	87	Riddle, Isabella	1886	75
Pritchard, Donald E.	1930	30	Riddle, James S.	1929	80
Pritchard, Eva M.	1986	93	Riddle, Pearl	1976	92
Pritchard, Jennie	1917	46	Riddle, S. Vance	1896	6
Pritchard, Samuel E.	1928	63	Robb, Bessie	1877	1
Pritchard, Samuel Earl	1930	41	Robb, Charles	1907	
Pritchard, Thomas A.	1982	91	Roberts	1914	Infant
Provost, Robert H.	1979	67	Roberts, John Brady	1926	64
Puch, Andrew	1921		Roberts, Joseph	1908	
Puhlman, Elizabeth	1989	72	Roberts, Junneth	1941	
Quinn	1931	Infant	Robinson, George	1867	77
Quinn, Bella Jane	1940		Robinson, James	1862	70
Quinn, Emma B.	1953	87	Robinson, Jean	1941	
Quinn, Hugh			Robinson, Nancy	1840	32
Quinn, Isabella			Robinson, Robert J.	1845	17
Quinn, John M.	1928	52	Rodger, William	1917	65
Quinn, Louisa			Ross, Daniel		
Quinn, Margaret	1875	54	Ross, Daniel	1834	7
Quinn, Martha	1891	28	Ross, James		
Quinn, William	1909	86	Ross, James	1838	8
Quinn, William J.	1936	75	Ross, James E.	1870	
Rankin, Samuel	1844	40	Ross, John	1846	12

Name	Died	Age	Name	Died	Age
Ross, Jonathon			Sangricco, Harry	1949	66
Ross, Mary			Sangricco, Harry E.	1947	11
Ross, Mary			Sarver, Anna	1920	
Ross, Mary			Sarver, Clyde	1902	19
Ross, Sarah A.	1845	16	Sarver, John	1917	
Rossell, Donald G.	1960	6	Sarver, Laura C.	1971	89
Rowe, Charlotte	1915	57	Sarver, Louis	1940	
Rowe, Francis McCoy	1949	65	Sarver, Mrs.	1910	
Rowe, Henry	1910		Sarver, Mrs.	1919	
Rowe, Henry	1947	68	Scalspi	1924	
Rowe, Joseph Sr.	1963	81	Scarborough, Mary C.	1880	58
Rowe, Lillian	1947	66	Scarborough, Virginia	1877	31
Rowe, Philip	1968	53	Schafer	1931	
Rowe, Robert	1980	73	Schafer, Emma E.	1928	
Rowe, Susie	1920		Schafer, John R.	1954	90
Rudolph, Ellen M	1989	93	Schafer, Louise L.	1945	47
Russ, Mayme	1946	48	Schafer, Ruth Hazel	1934	6
Russel, Mary	1908		Schafer, William L.	1974	75
Sample, Maurice E.	1955	65	Schaner, Emma R.	1956	
Sample, Nettie D.	1953	67	Schapman	1914	Infant
Sample, Shelby	1895	15	Schapman	1915	Infant
Sample, William C.	1899	42	Schapman, Pearl	1919	
Sampson	1912	Infant	Schapman, William	1919	
Sampson, Alexander	1843	9	Schofield, Roland C.	1957	Infant
Sampson, Elizabeth	1868	70	Schones, Peter	1937	72
Sampson, George	1910	70	Schons, Margaret	1956	85
Sampson, George	1921		Schrecengost	1924	Infant
Sampson, James P.	1936	52	Schrecengost, Annie	1963	65
Sampson, John	1873	75	Schrecengost, John	1922	
Sampson, John	1877	4	Schrecengost, John L.	1969	76
Sampson, Margaret	1910	66	Schrecengost, M.C.	1918	
Sampson, Mary	1873	37	Schrecengost, Samuel	1919	47
Sampson, Sarah	1867	80	Schrecengost, Samuel H.	1952	79
Sampson, Thomas L.	1874	3 Mo.	Schrecengost, Sarah Adelaide	1941	73
Sampson, William M.	1849	12	Schrock, Elmer E.	1956	86
Sampson, William K.	1873	7	Schrock, Maude C.	1947	70
Sangricco, Edward G.	1959	Infant	Schrock, Robert E.	1961	59
Sangricco, Emma	1963	80	Scott	1918	Infant

Appendix

Name	Died	Age	Name	Died	Age
Scott, Ada McDermitt	1936	79	Scott, Mattie Walker	1901	35
Scott, Alexander	1959	Infant	Scott, Nannie	1882	3
Scott, Anna K.	1969	74	Scott, Ralph W.	1901	1
Scott, Arabella Speer	1919	66	Scott, Ruth M.	1991	84
Scott, Catherine			Scott, Samuel		
Scott, Charles R.	1897	3	Scott, Samuel	1819	68
Scott, Charles W.	1957	74	Scott, Samuel	1888	73
Scott, Chester A.	1941	61	Scott, Samuel	1942	91
Scott, E. Pricilla	1903	47	Scott, Samuel Sr.	1829	40
Scott, Edward	1920		Scott, Samuel C.	1973	80
Scott, Elizabeth	1827	78	Scott, Samuel H.	1991	95
Scott, Elizabeth	1851	29	Scott, Sarah	1817	31
Scott, Elizabeth	1911	83	Scott, Sarah A.	1854	4
Scott, Ella P.	1956	76	Scott, Susie A.	1920	64
Scott, Elsie S.	1970	74	Scott, Thomas		
Scott, Fred P.	1981	71	Scott, Thomas	1820	12
Scott, Hays B.	1962	77	Scott, Wallace A.	1964	66
Scott, Ida R.	1976	82	Scott, Warren W.	1991	70
Scott, James H.	1986	54	Scott, William H. Sr.	1967	85
Scott, John	1901		Severns, Alice M.	1970	87
Scott, John	1902	61	Severns, Anna		
Scott, John	1906	81	Severns, Carrie	1977	73
Scott, John A.	1963	73	Severns, Catherine	1920	
Scott, John H.	1907	8	Severns, Kathryn	1932	
Scott, John P.	1933	70	Severns, Mr.	1908	
Scott, John R.	1971	46	Severns, Samuel T.	1954	96
Scott, John R. Sr.	1946	53	Severns, William F.	1968	63
Scott, Joseph	1867	70	Severns, William T.	1959	76
Scott, Leander	1866	12	Shaeffer, Carrie	1977	84
Scott, Maragaret B.	1989	68	Shafer, David	1907	37
Scott, Margaret A.	1849	15	Shafer, Elamer V.	1942	
Scott, Margaret E.	1971	85	Shafer, Mrs.	1910	68
Scott, Margaret U.	1964	64	Shafer, Theobold	1919	79
Scott, Mary			Shaner, C. A. Jr.	1913	87
Scott, Mary	1826	21	Shanner, Charles	1914	
Scott, Mary A.	1946	31	Sharp, Mr.	1902	
Scott, Mary A.	1975	89	Shaw, Archibald		
Scott, Mary J.	1851	3	Shaw, Elizabeth	1826	50

Name	Died	Age	Name	Died	Age
Shaw, Howard	1900		Sloan, George	1935	73
Shaw, Margaret A.	1876	60	Smart, Jonathan	1830	29
Sheldon, Elizabeth	1909		Smith, A. C.		
Sheldon, Frank	1910		Smith, Catharine		
Shellito, Fred C.	1953	88	Smith, Della J.		
Shellito, Lizzie J.	1941	67	Smith, Henry V.	1965	58
Sheridan, Abigial	1876	55	Smith, J. R.	1916	74
Sheridan, James	1886	73	Smith, James		
Sheridan, John Q.	1848	5	Smith, Margaret L.	1984	74
Shoemaker, Edith Briceland	1981	100	Smith, Mary A.		
Shones	1914	Infant	Smith, Mary J.		
Shones, Victor	1929	38	Smith, Mrs.	1916	
Shoup, Charles	1918	36	Smith, Robert		
Shoup, J. M.	1916	69	Smith, William		
Shoup, Jane	1918	64	Smokey, Anna V.	1962	61
Shoup, Pearl	1920	34	Snarey, John V.	1912	
Shuheider, John	1936	50	Snarey, Joseph A.	1957	75
Shulter, Donald	1929		Snary, Elizabeth Mae	1937	
Sigmond, Adolph	1932		Snary, Olive	1933	
Sigmond, John F.	1935	68	Spear, Absolom B.	1831	20
Sigmond, Mary	1944		Spear, Alexander	1865	56
Sigmond, Michael	1940		Spear, Andrew	1858	80
Sigmund, Amalia	1947	74	Spear, Andrew J.	1849	3
Sigmund, Frank Sr.	1968	67	Spear, Elizabeth	1857	86
Sigmund, Marg	1944	38	Spear, James	1858	
Sigmund, Maria	1968	98	Spear, Lafayette M.	1861	11 Mo.
Sigmund, Mollie	1969	64	Spear, Lizzie J.	1862	14
Simpson, Elizabeth B.	1958	70	Spear, William	1851	24
Simpson, Frances P.	1971	83	Speer, Andrew B.	1921	88
Simpson, George	1944		Speer, Blanche	1878	95
Simpson, James D.	1964	29	Speer, Clayton W.	1948	78
Simpson, Janet Burns	1932		Speer, Elizabeth	1878	
Simpson, Mark	1966	82	Speer, Elizabeth	1903	64
Simpson, Raymond P.	1971	63	Speer, Elizabeth	1912	77
Simpson, William R.	1971	88	Speer, Hannah	1907	86
Singer, Francis W.	1953	41	Speer, Walter B.	1906	28
Slagle	1912	Infant	Springer	1942	Infant
Slater, Emilie	1944		Springer, Marcella A.	1945	Infant

Appendix 121

Name	Died	Age	Name	Died	Age
Sproat, Andrew	1863	53	Stewart, Samuel A.	1970	48
Sproat, David	1895	77	Stewart, Sarah A.	1863	1
Sproat, Louise	1898	58	Stewart, Susannah V.	1945	90
Stafford, Suzanna	1962	83	Stewart, Thomas E.	1918	73
Standish, Frank	1932		Stewart, Walter	1903	42
Standish, Henry S.	1894	38	Stewart, William	1902	
Standish, Jane	1930		Still, Benjamin	1871	77
Standish, Sarah E.	1923	67	Still, John	1850	59
Standish, Vesta	1939	31	Stockdale, Eliza Ann	1907	80
Stankevich	1955	Infant	Stone, Charles	1911	3
Stark, Margaret E.	1985	70	Stone, Edward	1898	4
Stavropoulas	1970	Infant	Stone, Luther W.	1953	95
Sterrett, Andrew J.	1862	26	Stone, Maude S.	1927	58
Stevenson, Susannah	1857	44	Stoner, Arley	1988	75
Stevenson, Willie	1859	40	Strahan, Grazzilla		
Stewart, Anna M.	1924	61	Strahan, Isaac		
Stewart, Celestia D.	1988	71	Strahan, Mary		
Stewart, Charles E.	1969	75	Strang	1903	Infant
Stewart, Elizabeth	1863	40	Strang, David	1942	71
Stewart, Harry L.	1981	94	Strang, Ellen D.	1937	71
Stewart, Isaac J.	1874	57	Strang, William A.	1854	60
Stewart, James	1894	1	Tacy, Claris F.	1965	65
Stewart, James A.	1917	58	Tacy, Freda V.	1987	85
Stewart, James H.	1952	72	Tate, Elizabeth	1857	39
Stewart, James R. Sr.	1992	53	Taylor, John	1980	78
Stewart, Jane	1863	95	Taylor, John W.	1943	67
Stewart, Jane	1900	82	Taylor, John W.	1948	47
Stewart, Jennie E.	1987	90	Taylor, Margaret M.	1956	82
Stewart, John	1854	61	Thomas, Cecil	1986	75
Stewart, John	1904	61	Thomas, Sarah A.	1968	83
Stewart, Lizzie W.	1863	5	Thornburg, Diana	1850	70
Stewart, Maggie A.	1863	2	Thornburg, Elizabeth	1836	37
Stewart, Margaret	1862	73	Thornburg, Jacob	1883	101
Stewart, Martha S.	1942		Thornburg, Jane	1846	19
Stewart, Mary	1854	29	Thornburg, Jane	1869	80
Stewart, Nancy J.	1838	10	Thornburg, John		
Stewart, Robert	1959	78	Thornburg, Mrs.	1907	
Stewart, Samuel	1837	7	Thornburg, Nevada		

Name	Died	Age	Name	Died	Age
Thornburg, Rebecca			Turnbull, Thomas H. Jr.	1992	76
Thornburg, Samuel	1878		Turnbull, Thomas H. Sr.	1956	69
Thornburg, Thomas		16	Turner, Charolette E.	1921	
Thornburg, Thomas	1855	86	Tyson, Charles	1943	
Tidball	1837	Infant	Tyson, Virginia	1938	26
Tidball, A. Howard	1881	3	Uffelman, Charles	1921	Infant
Tidball, Cassandria	1877	51	Uffelman, Florence B.	1977	84
Tidball, Elizabeth	1849	45	Uffelman, Nickolas	1973	86
Tidball, Elizabeth	1882	79	Uffelman, William	1919	1
Tidball, James E.	1939	74	Underwood, James J.	1973	70
Tidball, James N.	1891	62	Underwood, Theresa A.	1971	66
Tidball, Jennie M.	1965	84	Verner	1919	Infant
Tidball, John M.		Infant	Verner	1922	Infant
Tidball, Levina	1886	39	Verner	1930	Infant
Tidball, Margaret	1981	80	Verner, Charlotte E.	1971	75
Tidball, Mary E.	1947	85	Verner, Dalton E.	1980	62
Tidball, Merle H.	1969	65	Verner, Dalton W.	1965	70
Tidball, Vance W.	1881	1	Verner, David	1916	62
Tidball, William	1844	40	Verner, Effie A.	1945	73
Tidball, William Esq.	1884	88	Verner, Ewing J.	1958	62
Tidball, William F.	1943	73	Verner, James	1900	49
Tidball, William M.	1993	65	Verner, John P.	1945	86
Tidball, Wilson G.	1972	74	Verner, Lucy	1947	56
Torrence, Albert	1840	66	Verner, Mary A.	1991	90
Torrence, James			Verner, Norman R.	1944	23
Torrence, James M. D.	1865	79	Verner, Sophia	1903	74
Torrence, Jane N.	1878	71	Verner, William	1929	72
Torrence, M.D. Albert	1904	78	Wagner	1927	Infant
Torrence, Mattie			Wagner, Bessie B.	1948	60
Torrence, Minnie			Wagner, Elizabeth S.	1972	77
Towers, Margaret W.	1991	87	Wagner, Francis	1936	82
Towers, William C.	1977	73	Wagner, James J.	1991	75
Trexler, Mary	1942		Wagner, Mary	1932	
Tuminski, Delma J.	1967	37	Wagner, Otho N.	1969	78
Turnbull, Arlene G.	1987	65	Walker, Ella	1940	
Turnbull, Frank W.	1980	51	Walker, Gabriel	1799	64
Turnbull, Howard	1932		Walker, Gabriel	1862	78
Turnbull, James E.	1924		Walker, Issac	1812	66

Appendix

Name	Died	Age	Name	Died	Age
Walker, James	1895	82	White, Mary B.	1968	95
Walker, James	1918	74	White, Mildred	1945	31
Walker, James Sr.	1845	76	White, Robinson	1942	69
Walker, Jane	1850	70	Whiteford, Robert	1930	
Walker, Julia A.	1904	85	Whiteford, Robert E.	1979	41
Walker, Margaret	1815	75	Wildey, Clarence	1934	57
Walker, Margaret	1859	87	Wildey, Mary A.	1963	85
Walker, Mary	1845	28	Wildey, Stella E.	1907	1
Walker, Mary	1853	37	Williams, David A.	1990	45
Walker, Mary J.	1855	14	Williams, Jane Ewing	1910	
Walker, Mr.	1902		Wilson, Isabella	1934	59
Walker, Novella A.	1958	81	Wilson, Robert	1949	77
Walker, Rebecca	1862	80	Wilson, Willis Wayne	1941	
Walker, Robert B.	1935	64	Winning, Alexander W.	1958	67
Wallock, Amelia	1924		Winning, Robert	1947	26
Wallock, Amelia	1925		Winters, Charles	1922	
Walls	1926	Infant	Woollett, Agnes G.	1993	87
Walsh, Mary	1934	62	Woollett, Clara B.	1956	78
Walton, George	1918	44	Woollett, John D.	1949	
Walton, James H.	1923		Woollett, John D.	1979	74
Walton, Thomas	1923	54	Woollett, Karen	1961	2
Watson		Infant	Woollett, Kelly Marie	1986	15
Watson		Infant	Woollett, Marie A.	1966	61
Watson, David	1916		Wright, Laura W.	1950	
Watson, Edward D.	1891		Wright, Michael		
Watson, Mrs.	1911		Wright, Sarah H.	1959	75
Watson, Samuel B.	1917		Young	1921	Infant
Watson, William			Young, Abigal	1860	83
Watt, Agnes	1825	29	Young, Basel W.	1833	Infant
Watt, Andrew	1838	75	Young, D. G. W.	1862	21
Watt, Elleanor	1839	76	Young, E. J.	1908	
Watt, Elleanor J.	1845	5	Young, Elizabeth		
Watt, John	1800	3	Young, F. W. H.	1860	2
Watt, Philander	1839	2	Young, Guy F.	1904	2
Wembish, John	1928		Young, Hannah		
White, Barbara Sue	1953	1	Young, James S.	1814	11
White, Edith W.	1949	25	Young, Jean	1936	
White, Margaret E.	1987	48	Young, Johanna	1853	16

Name	Died	Age	Name	Died	Age
Young, John	1857	15	Young, Marian A.	1901	1
Young, John Jr.	1872	70	Young, Mary	1859	
Young, John Sr.	1853	80	Young, Matthew	1817	21
Young, John F.	1904	36	Young, P. M.	1838	
Young, John J.	1864	21	Young, Raymond	1899	2
Young, John M.	1834	6 mo.	Young, Samuel	1898	83
Young, Joseph	1838	29	Young, Sarah J.	1846	1
Young, LaVerne	1921	18	Young, William H.	1865	30
Young, Lizzie E.	1881	28			

Appendix E
Church Officers (1774-1993)

This appendix lists, as best we have found them written, the elders, deacons, and trustees that have served Union Presbyterian Church since its beginning. The column **Year** in the table below represents the year when the individual was first elected/installed into the position (NK means Not Known). Persons serving more than one term are only listed once. A number in parenthesis after a name indicates two different individuals with the same name held the office.

ELDERS		DEACONS		TRUSTEES	
Name	Year	Name	Year	Name	Year
Walker, Isaac	1794	Adams, Wm.	1894	Hall, John	1811
Marks, William Sr.	1794	Donald, Leonard	1894	Phillips, Jonathon	1811
Phillips, Johnathan (1)	1794	Phillips, Wm. J.	1894	McKee, George	1811
McMichael, Isaac	1794	McCurdy, J. Andrew	1894	Glass, Sam'l	1834
McCormick, James	1823	Phillips, Sam'l	1894	Phillips, Alexander	1834
McMichael, John Jr.	1823	Unknown - Disbanded	NK	Phillips, Thos.	1834
Stewart, Samuel	NK	Tidball, Wilson	1953	McCormick, William G.	1834
McKee, George	1835	Elliott, Chester	1953	McCormick, Hugh	1834
Phillips, Alexander Sr.	1835	Person, Otto	1953	McKee, David	1834
Glass, Samuel Sr.	1835	Grace, Harold	1953	Hall, William	1834
Hall, William	1835	Fry, Charles Jr.	1953	Phillips, Alexander Jr.	1846
Watt, William	1835	Karns, Frank	1953	Scott, Jos.	1846
Boyd, Joseph	1838	Puhlman, Charles Jr.	1953	Ross, Jas.	1846
Marks, William Jr.	1838	Turner, V.A.	1953	Harbison, Matthew Jr.	1847
Phillips, Samuel	1850	McCullough, Raymond	1953	Ewing, Samuel W.	1849
Dickson, Andrew	1850	Hamilton, J. Ray	1953	Hall, Mat.	1850
Glass, William	1858	Davis, Wm. W.	1953	Phillips, John S.	1852
Phillips, John S.	1858	Parkison, Wm W. Sr.	1953	McCurdy, Jos.	1852
Spear, Alexander	1858	Baer, Donnis	1955	Ewing, Isaac A.	1853
McCoy, William	1858	Hutchison, Virgil M.	1955	Scott, Samuel	1855
Benton, Thomas	1858	Malarky, Francis	1955	McKee, George Y.	1856
Phillips, Johnathan (2)	1869	Mitchell, Samuel	1955	Ekin, Wm.	1857
Scott, Samuel	1869	Wilson, Elliott	1955	Brown, Hugh	1858
Aiken, Johnathan	1869	White, Herbert	1956	Ewing, Nellson	1858
McKendry, Andrew	1869	Wagner, James	1956	Ewing, Isaac	1859
McCurdy, Joseph J.	1881	Forsyth, W. Stuart	1956	Nichol, John	1860
Scott, John	1881	Nelson, Clifford G.	1956	Speer, Andrew B.	1861
Aiken, James	1892	McKenzie, William	1956	McMichael, James	1861
Phillips, John W.	1892	Headly, Edwin K.	1957	Scott, Hugh	1862
Phillips, Milton S.	1903	Miltenberger, Clyde	1957	Speer, Andrew	1864
Scott, J. Walter	1903	Phillips, Robert W.	1957	Clark, Wm. H.	1865
Scott, John P.	1903	McGeary, John	1957	McCormick, B.	1866
McCurdy, J. Andrew	1911	Rex, Donald	1957	Aikin, Jonathon	1867
Phillips, Frank H.	1911	Pfaub, Robert H.	1958	Glass, Hugh	1869
Glass, Albert P.	1911	Cox, J. Authur	1958	Phillips, John M.	1870
Speer, Clayton W.	1925	Lloyd, William	1958	McMichael, J.R.	1871

ELDERS		DEACONS		TRUSTEES	
Name	Year	Name	Year	Name	Year
Scott, Charles W.	1925	Silver, James L. Sr.	1958	McCluskey, Henry	1873
Pritchard, Samuel E.	1925	Boyd, Charles	1958	Campbell, Alex.	1874
Elliot, James	1925	Redding, Carl	1959	McCurdy, J.J.	1875
Phillips, Andrew H.	1929	Gray, George	1959	Scott, John	1878
Adams, Percy L.	1929	Fraysier, Henry	1959	Bell, Hays	1879
Shellito, Fred	1934	Deemer, Jerry	1959	Speer, Geo.	1882
Neely, William	1934	Adamczak, Eugene	1959	Dickson, Samuel	1882
McMichael, John C.	1934	Gonze, Charles	1959	Adams, Wm.	1883
McCurdy, Joseph D.	1934	Houghton, Vernon	1959	Glass, H.M.	1884
Bell, W. Wallace	1934	McKean, James	1959	Aiken, Wm.	1885
Glass, Leonard D.	1942	Uffelman, Robert C.	1959	Phillips, W.S.	1885
McCormick, James S.	1942	Smith, Thomas E.	1961	Glass, Hugh M.	1886
Glass, William H.	1942	Yamber, Stephen	1961	Phillips, M.S.	1888
Marshall, Howard L.	1948	Trautman, G. Warren	1961	Adams, John	1889
Hutchison, Virgil	1948	Bauman, Edward E.	1962	Scott, John P.	1893
Phillips, Howard S.	1948	Mawhinney, Warren	1962	Scott, J. P.	1895
Glass, William D.	1948	Scott, R. Donald	1962	Bell, J. H.	1903
Kinney, Charles E.	1953	Glas, Wm. H. Jr.	1962	Adams, W. A.	1907
LeSuer, Charles E.	1953	Fry, Charles E. Jr.	1962	Phillips, W. J.	1907
McCormick, Wm. A. Jr.	1953	Hicks, Paul J. Jr.	1964	McCurdy, Andrew	1907
Patterson, Vernon C.	1953	Kropf, Robert	1964	McCoy, W. J.	1907
Miltenberger, Clyde E.	1957	Moroz, Alex J.	1964	Aiken, James	1908
Morrow, Craig C.	1957	Robinson, W. Negley	1964	McCurdy, A.	1909
Mitchell, Samuel J.	1959	Ecoff, Walter C.	1965	Scott, Howard	1911
Pfaub, Robert H.	1959	Glass, Robert G.	1965	Scott, Wm. H.	1911
Redding, Carl	1959	Howard, John E.	1965	McCormick, W. A.	1912
McGeary, John D.	1959	Oldham, Richard K.	1965	McKenzie, Thomas	1912
Provost, Robert H.	1961	Puhlman, Charles R. Sr.	1965	Phillips, C. K.	1913
Cox, J. Arthur	1961	Blair, Gilbert	1966	Phillips, Howard	1916
Forsyth, W. Stuart	1961	Brammer, Mrs. L.F. (Helen)	1966	Guyser, Fred	1917
Fry, Charles E. Sr.	1961	Miles, John H.	1966	McCoy, Wm.	1918
Briggs, Robert E.	1962	Phillips, Mrs Howard S (Anna)	1966	Cook, Gregg	1919
Gray, George A.	1962	Harbaugh, George	1967	Campbell, Harper	1919
Nelson, Clifford	1962	Gettemy, George	1967	Scott, Wm.	1920
Person, Otto F.	1962	McCullough, Raymond Jr.	1967	Andrews, Mark	1920
Silver, James L. Sr.	1962	Macek, Roy	1967	Shellito, T.C.	1922
Phillips, Robert W.	1964	Campbell, C. John	1968	Scott, Russell	1922
Sarver, James R.	1964	Glass, Mrs. Wm D. S. (Nellie)	1968	Rowe, Frank	1923
Gonze, Charles D.	1965	Phillips, G. Scott	1968	Campbell, Scott	1925
Fry, Charles E. Jr.	1966	Brown, Margaret	1969	Clever, Martin	1926
Boyd, Charles	1967	Jackson, Stanley	1969	Williams, Charles	1927
Gibb, James	1967	Kriss, Andrew	1969	Scott, John R.	1928
Grgurich, Joseph	1967	Parker, Robert F.	1969	Linton, Samuel	1928
Sherockman, Andrew A. Dr.	1968	Kuehn, E. Gary	1970	Scott, Frank	1929
Deemer, Arthur W.	1969	Pearce, Mrs. Henry (Jessie)	1970	Neely, Wm. G.	1930
Fraysier, Henry	1969	Shakely, Mrs Howard (Caroline)	1970	Glass, Leonard	1931
Ifft, Charles	1969	Preg, Stephen Michael Jr.	1970	McMichael, John	1933

Appendix

ELDERS		DEACONS		TRUSTEES	
Name	Year	Name	Year	Name	Year
Karns, Frank	1969	Fitzpatrick, James W.	1970	Neely, Wm.	1933
Lloyd, William	1970	Macek, Mrs John Jr (Donna)	1971	McCormick, James	1933
Trautman, G. Warren	1970	Schild, Roger A.	1971	Scott, Hays	1934
Glass, Robert G.	1971	McCormick, Eleanor	1971	Tacy, Howard	1935
Parker, Robert F.	1971	Barish, Joseph M.	1972	Scott, Albert	1937
Franz, Robert W.	1972	Jenkins, Charles E.	1972	Harper, Jack	1938
Howard, John E.	1972	Timberlake, A. Gerald	1972	Pearson, Mr.	1939
Preg, S. Michael Jr.	1972	Heasley, Raymond E. Jr.	1973	Learish, D. E.	1939
Fitzpatrick, James W.	1973	Wickline, George J.	1973	Zug, Fred	1940
Macek, Roy M.	1973	Butler, Wm. J. Jr.	1973	Scott, Wallace	1942
Oldham, Richard K.	1973	Jones, Robert D.	1973	McCormick, John	1942
Schild, Roger A.	1973	Morley, Richard	1973	Deemer, Jerry	1942
Campbell, C. John	1974	Stewart, James R. Sr.	1973	Mitchell, Samuel	1943
Campbell, Matthew	1975	Higgs, E. Warren	1973	Patterson, Vernon	1944
Scott, R. Donald	1975	Suehr, Peter R.	1973	Learish, Earl	1947
Hopper, Clair	1975	Boyd, Mrs. Chas. S.	1974	Glass, Wm.	1948
Coulter, James L. Sr.	1976	Feathers, Valerie	1974	Provost, Robert	1948
Jackson, Stanley B.	1976	Janney, Alan	1974	Wilson, James	1950
Lowery, Kenneth G.	1976	Coulter, Jas. L. Sr.	1974	Kinney, C. E.	1950
Gettemy, George C.	1978	Elias, Edward N.	1975	Glass, Wm. D.	1951
Uffelman, H. Glenn	1978	Fitzpatrick, Wm. M.	1975	McCormick, Benjamin	1952
Puhlman, Charles R. Jr.	1979	Peters, Edward L.	1975	Kinney, Elmer	1953
Lucht, Paul G.	1980	Murphy, Michael D.	1975	Scott, Warren	1953
Phillips, Jacob L. Jr.	1980	Lautanen, Robert O.	1975	Briggs, Robert	1954
Trinkala, John W.	1980	Uffelman, Kathleen	1975	Malarky, Francis	1954
Pfaub, Jacqueline (Mrs. R.H.)	1980	Houghton, Vernon T. Jr.	1975	Cox, J. Authur	1955
Pearce, Jessie G.	1981	Wagner, James N.	1975	Morrow, Craig	1956
Wickline, George J.	1981	Myers, Mrs Oliver D (Evelyn)	1976	Rogers, George	1958
Connor, Arletta M.	1981	Rich, Roland	1976	Karns, Frank	1960
Noble, Ethelyn B.	1982	Wilson, Peter R.	1977	Towers, William	1961
Rich, Roland J.	1982	Hopper, Samuel W.	1977	Boyd, Charles	1961
Snead, M. Paul	1982	Lucht, Paul	1977	Grgurich, Joseph	1962
Anderson, Kenneth A.	1983	Kunselman, Larry	1978	Hopper, Clair	1962
Deemer, Marion K.	1983	Andrews, Mrs. Donald (Sally)	1979	Uffelman, Glenn	1963
Willoughby, John A.	1984	Scott, Jeffrey L.	1979	Lloyd, William	1963
Dorsch, Carl J.	1984	Scott, John H.	1979	Wagner, James	1964
Ganser, Scott D.	1985	Christopher, Mrs. Ruth J.	1980	LeSuer, Charles	1964
Scott, Doris W.	1985	Cochenour, Terry K.	1980	Irwin, James	1965
Strunk, James F. Sr.	1985	Rumbaugh, James L.	1980	Porter, Paul	1965
Cochenour, Terry K.	1985	Winning, Robert G.	1980	Hershelman, Kenneth	1966
Holczer, Thomas J.	1985	Strunk, James F. Sr.	1980	Puhlman, Chas. R. Jr.	1966
Jukes, Ellen K.	1986	Aleski, Shirley A.	1981	Roush, Guy K.	1967
Kuehn, Bonnie K.	1986	Ifft, Charles C.	1981	Scott, James H.	1967
Scott, Jeffrey L.	1987	Jones, Douglas E.	1981	Howard, John E.	1968
Lenz, Raymond C.	1987	McCormick, Kathryn E.	1981	Scott, R. Donald	1970
Howard, Ethel E.	1987	Quinn, Carol G.	1981	McCormick, John S.	1971
Coulter, Nancy C.	1989	Jones, Denise E.	1982	Cue, Cameron T. Jr.	1972

ELDERS		DEACONS		TRUSTEES	
Name	**Year**	**Name**	**Year**	**Name**	**Year**
DeMaddis, W. Russell	1989	Willoughby, John A.	1982	Tacy, Elick	1972
Thomas, Kathy E.	1989	Gray, Gary G.	1983	English, Clyde A.	1973
Ballantine, Bruce A.	1990	Backinger, Patricia A.	1983	Phillips, Jacob L. Jr.	1973
Davis, Scott K.	1991	Espy, William N.	1983	Yamber, Stephen	1976
Scott, Cathleen C.	1991	Sparbanie, Gladys F.	1983	Panazzi, Ernest A.	1977
Clemenson, Michelle L.	1992	Jukes, Donald E.	1984	Tidball, William M.	1978
DiClemente, Carol C.	1992	Holczer, Thomas J.	1985	Herbert, John	1979
Hopper, Samuel W.	1992	Stewart, Beverly	1985	Miles, John H. Sr.	1979
Andrews, Sally J.	1993	Wickline, Karla	1985	Lenz, Raymond C.	1981
Gazda, Elizabeth J.	1993	Kamenar, Paul K.	1985	Aleski, Shirley E.	1982
		Clemenson, Michelle L.	1986	Wickline, George J.	1984
		DiClemente, Carol C.	1986	Murphy, Michael D.	1985
		Ganser, Linda L.	1986	Kuehn, E. Gary	1986
		Whiteman, Michael W. Jr.	1986	Ball, George H.	1986
		Lanigan, Charles D.	1987	Cue, Nicholas J.	1987
		Reed, Carl L.	1987	Jones, Douglas E.	1987
		Salvitti, Charles J.	1987	Lang, Cheryl Irwin	1989
		Thomas, Kathy E.	1987	Pecharka, David M.	1990
		Campbell, Carole	1988	Jukes, Donald E.	1991
		Menni, Jody H.	1988	Scott, Jeffrey L.	1991
		Schienle, Catherine A.	1988	Simon, Jeffrey Z.	1992
		Lickovich, Sally A.	1989		
		Parrish, Ronald L.	1989		
		Phillips, Rachel I.	1989		
		Martin, Douglas L.	1990		
		Waszyn, Andrew A.	1990		
		Connell, Thomas R.	1991		
		Diskin, Dorothy A.	1991		
		Harmasch, Carla J.	1991		
		Freemire, Susan E.	1992		
		Kennedy, Michael S.	1992		
		Miles, Bonnie E.	1992		
		Cain, Cynthia J.	1993		
		DeMaddis, W. Russell	1993		
		Kamenar, Patricia A.	1993		
		Poppelreiter, Susan	1993		